LOTTERY SUPER SYSTEM

AVERY CARDOZA

LOTTERY SUPER SYSTEM

AVERY CARDOZA

CARDOZA PUBLISHING

Cardoza Publishing is the foremost gaming and gambling publisher in the world with a library of almost 200 up-to-date and easy-to-read books and strategies. These authoritative works are written by the top experts in their fields and with more than 10 million books in print, represent the best-selling and most popular gaming books anywhere.

FIRST EDITION

Copyright © 2016 by Avery Cardoza
All Rights Reserved

Library of Congress Catalog Number: 2013946691
ISBN 10: 1-58042-324-8   ISBN 13: 978-1-58042-324-3

Visit our new web site (www.cardozabooks.com) or write us for a full list of books, advanced and computer strategies.

CARDOZA PUBLISHING

P.O. Box 98115, Las Vegas, NV 89193
Toll Free Phone (800)577-WINS
email: cardozabooks@aol.com
www.cardozabooks.com

ABOUT THE AUTHOR

Avery Cardoza, the world's foremost authority on gambling and a million-selling author of more than 40 books and advanced strategies, is the founder of Cardoza Publishing (publisher of more than 200 gaming titles, 10 million copies sold) and owner of the legendary Gambler's Book Club in Las Vegas. Millions of gamblers have learned how to play and win money at gambling following his no-nonsense practical advice.

Cardoza has been studying numbers, and winning systems since he was five-years old. He has developed the most powerful lottery software and strategies ever formulated including the only systems using powerful Level II keys such as kings, wizards, and courts, and Level III advanced strategies found nowhere else. Cardoza is one of the foremost experts on predictive randomness for lotteries, the heart and soul of strategies that have won players millions of dollars. The result of his lifetime efforts in mathematics, gambling, and random occurrences is *Lottery Super System*, the most authoritative book on beating lottery and lotto that has ever been written.

Cardoza's work is also the centerpiece of LotterySuperSystem.com, the powerful online site for casual and serious players looking to win millions of dollars at lottery and lotto games.

To Kevin Thornton

TABLE OF CONTENTS

SECTION I
FOUNDATION

SECTION II
TOOLS, ANALYSES, STRATEGIES

SECTION III
WHEELS

SECTION IV
ADVANCED STRATEGIES

SECTION V
THE COMPLETE LOTTERY PLAYER

SECTION I

FOUNDATION

1

INTRODUCTION

You can win money at the lottery! Many millionaires out there will attest to that. And more people are becoming millionaires all the time. You never know, you may be the next super million-dollar lottery winner. It has happened and it can happen again. All your dreams can come true—becoming wealthy, traveling the world, doing anything you want.

I'd like you to be one of the few who catches that dream.

I'm going to teach you how to approach lottery and lotto games with a solid plan. You'll learn more about beating these games than you ever imagined possible. Much of the information and winning secrets revealed to you in this book have never been published before, either publicly or privately. *Lottery Super System* is jam-packed cover to cover with powerful strategies specifically designed to beat lottery and lotto games. You'll learn the powerful Level I core strategies, the Level II strategies with the mighty keys, and how to combine these two levels into juggernaut Level III strategies.

Lottery Super System is the most complete book ever written on beating lottery and lotto games. Many new strategies and approaches are revealed here for the very first time. You'll learn how to use dual-master and rotating-master keys to beat multi-state games like Powerball and Mega Millions, plus specific strategies to beat three-ball and four-ball lotteries, five-ball and six-ball lotto, and how to use wheels to optimize your best-performing numbers.

You'll learn how to create chosen numbers and work with all the core analyses—best number, overdue, cluster and many more. You'll also learn how to combine these with kings, queens, wizards, earls, dukes, courts, lucky numbers and other advanced Level II keys to attack every major lottery and lotto game available with the super powerful Level III strategies. There is much, much more—from the odds and valuable playing tips to computer strategies and money management.

I also reveal the important secrets that every successful lottery player must know to win jackpots in any lottery or lotto game in the U.S., Canada, or anywhere else in the world.

If you're looking to beat the lottery by using birthdays, anniversaries, and the moon charts, and if you think everything in life is random, this is the wrong book for you. Becoming a winner at lottery and lotto games takes work, it takes strategies, and it takes luck. People win all the time. In this book, I help you get off the sidelines and into the game by taking you to the next level.

My real goal is for you to win millions and millions of dollars playing lottery and lotto games.

2

OVERVIEW

I cover a lot of important material in this book, taking you from the very basics of the games and the psychology of winning all the way through to advanced winning strategies, practical wisdom, money management, and how to practically and psychologically handle what you're shooting for—winning a huge jackpot.

This chapter is a preview of the book's topics to help you understand how you're going to attack lottery and lotto games to reach your goals.

CHAPTER PREVIEW

Chapter 1: Introduction
You've already read Chapter 1 and now know the goal of this book—showing you how to win millions of dollars playing lottery and lotto games.

Chapter 2: Overview
In this chapter, I go over the important topics that I cover in this book. You also get a very broad look at how to create winning tickets.

Chapter 3: The Winning Mindset
The mental aspects of trying to beat any form of gambling, including lottery and lotto games, are critical to winning.

This chapter examines the importance of taking a winning approach and keeping a positive attitude in trying to beat the numbers games.

Chapter 4: Overview of Lottery and Lotto Games

You'll learn the differences between lottery and lotto games, and learn about the many types of games available—instant games, three-ball and four-ball lottery, five-ball and six-ball lotto, and the dual-pool, multi-state games with huge jackpots.

Chapter 5: The Theory of Beating the Lottery

This chapter touches on the math behind the lottery, understanding and recognizing bias, and the philosophy behind the strategies we're going to use. We look at a small series of coin flips, the simplest example of trends, and show how we can use that thinking in lottery prediction analysis.

Chapter 6: Strategy Overview

We take a very brief look at the Level I, Level II and Level III strategies as a precursor to a deeper investigation in the three subsequent chapters, and learn the important concepts of chosen numbers, confidence level and regression analysis.

Chapter 7: Level I Play: The Core Strategies

The Level I core strategies are at the heart of all winning strategies. We carefully go over the basic analysis tools, charts and methods we'll use to beat lottery and lotto games—positional analysis, Best Number Analysis, Overdue Number Analysis, cluster analysis, frequency analysis, and the concept of weighting numbers.

Chapter 8: Level II Strategies: Key Numbers

You'll learn how to build on the strength of Level I strategies and chosen numbers, plus the various keys and their importance in advanced strategies—master, major, minor, and third keys. You'll also learn about kings, queens, dukes, earls, courts and working with lucky numbers (big luck, little luck, side luck).

Chapter 9: Wheeling Strategy

This very important chapter illustrates the value of playing wheels, and shows you how to align your Level I core-strategy chosen numbers into powerful ticket combinations. You also learn the cost of playing every chosen number and how to make a wheel template.

Chapter 10: Wheels & Key Numbers

To bring out the full power of the various types of keys requires prudent use of wheels for full coverage of chosen numbers and keys, and for efficiency in making tickets. We dig deeply into this subject and also cover under-wheeling, over-wheeling, and how to improve your odds by using the Big Wheel strategy.

Chapter 11: Three-Ball & Four-Ball Level III Lottery Strategies

You now apply the strategies you have learned into powerful Level III strategies specifically designed for three-ball and four-ball lottery games. You also learn how to play single tickets and multiple tickets, and combine keys with hot numbers, overdue numbers, and other chosen numbers (including lucky numbers) into optimal wheels.

Chapter 12: Five-Ball & Six-Ball
Level III Lotto Strategies

All the knowledge you have learned for finding chosen numbers and identifying keys comes together for a concerted Level III attack on lotto games. We leverage the core strategies and keys to form powerful tickets aimed at winning jackpots.

Chapter 13: Dual-Pool
Level III Lottery Game Strategies

The dual-pool, multi-state games like Powerball and Mega Millions offer jackpots that reach the hundreds of millions of dollars. You'll learn how to analyze and attack the dual pools using Level III strategies, how to decipher results, and how to use dual-master and rotating-master keys to chase big jackpot wins.

Chapter 14: The Financial Plan

The major concept of this chapter is how to be smart with your money—and it may well be the most important chapter in this book. Careful and in-depth discussions on the amount you should bet on tickets or invest overall, what to do if you win the big one and, most important of all, money management are the essential strategies you need to become a successful lottery or lotto player.

Chapter 15: The Odds of Winning

This chapter gives you a practical and theoretical look at the various aspects of the odds you face at lottery and lotto games, including the odds of hitting jackpots in various lotto games, Powerball and Mega Millions, how the number of balls in a lotto pool affect your chances of hitting a jackpot, and some sage and candid advice on playing multiplier bets in dual-pool multi-state games.

Chapter 16. 7 Ways to Increase Your Winning Chances or Percentage of Return

I show you seven ways to increase your winning chances or percentage of return, provide a straightforward look at the realities of playing, and end with an interesting discussion of "the reds and the greens."

Chapter 17: 10 Valuable Playing Tips

We'll cover 10 important playing tips, some of which have not previously been discussed in this book, some of which are worth repeating, and all of which are helpful or essential toward supporting your goal of beating lottery and lotto games.

Chapter 18: Practical Wisdom & Further Thoughts

I give you more useful and essential tips on winning, including a discussion of the best strategies for beating lottery and lotto games; how to choose games; how much money you should spend weekly on tickets; and how long before you should expect results. I also discuss "foolproof" strategies and playing less-chosen numbers.

Chapter 19: Beating Lottery and Lotto with Your Computer

With computers and computer software specifically programmed to beat lottery and lotto games, beating the numbers games has never been easier. We talk a little about my free online strategy program, www.lotterysupersystem.com.

Chapter 20: Go Get 'Em

This chapter is my last chance to send you on your way with a positive message and wish you great luck. May the wind be behind you!

Glossary of Important Terms & Concepts

Refresh your memory or look up the concepts and terms discussed throughout this book, from chosen numbers and keys to side luck and kings.

HOW TO MAKE WINNING TICKETS

Here, in broad strokes, is what you will do in your quest to pick winning lottery and lotto tickets. Follow these seven steps:

1. Choose Your Game

You often have a range of games from which to choose. In just about every state, you have a choice of playing the multi-state Powerball, Mega Millions and other similar games. in addition to the local state games. If you live near a state border, you also have the option of playing another state's games as well. Find the game you like, the one that's most comfortable for you, and that's the game you should play. Or play several games regularly.

2. Choose Your Strategy

You have many strategies to choose from. You can stick with one as your main strategy, combine several together, or even alternate among various options. If you're using computer software such as lotterysupersystem.com, you can use your favorite available strategy or combine several together to automatically generate numbers according to the parameters you set.

3. Choose Your Numbers

Once you choose your strategy, you will generate a pool of numbers to work with. Or if you are using an online program, it will automatically generate the best-performing balls for your analysis. Either on paper or with software, you'll choose which analysis to extract data from, and the length of history for tracking and interpreting results.

4. Choose the Number of Tickets You Want to Play

The more tickets you choose the more it costs, so you want to select a reasonable number of tickets for your budget. Your decision for how many tickets to purchase starts and ends with money management concepts and practical circumstances.

5. Wheel Your Numbers to Get the Most Efficient Coverage Possible

The wheeling systems will create the best wheels for the numbers you choose and the number of tickets you wish to play.

6. Buy Your Tickets

Your strategies have called out the right numbers for you to play. Using that information, get the requisite number of tickets you've outlined in your strategy.

7. Get Results

When the drawing occurs, hope that you've chosen well! Of course, there's always another drawing to attack!

HOW TO MAKE WINNING TICKETS
7 Steps to Picking Winning Tickets

1. Choose Your Game
2. Choose Your Strategy
3. Choose Your Numbers
4. Choose the Number of Tickets You Want to Play
5. Wheel Your Numbers to Get the Most Efficient Coverage Possible
6. Buy Your Tickets
7. Get Results

3

THE WINNING MINDSET

THE IMPORTANCE OF A WINNING APPROACH

Buying lottery and lotto tickets based on hunches, horoscopes, numerology, oracles, wavelengths and whatever other random beliefs are approaches based on, well…nothing. There is no plan at all, just a Hail Mary shot in the dark with no methodology whatsoever. You may have been guilty of this yourself on occasion, but obviously, you're reading this book because you want a real plan.

If you want to win, you need a concerted approach and you need to put forth some effort. The strategies don't work all by themselves—you have to do some figuring and make some decisions. Using my strategies won't be the hardest thing you've ever done, but it does require effort and a bit of strategic thinking. To get ahead, you need to do more than average players who may as well pick their numbers out of a hat.

As the old saying goes, "If it were that easy, everyone would be doing it."

THE IMPORTANCE OF POSITIVE ATTITUDE

Cynics might say that attitude doesn't change the odds in lottery, that a ticket is a ticket. Okay, that's a particular viewpoint. You could just as easily say that about a number of things in life. And sure, once you buy the ticket, a ticket *is* a ticket, and how you feel about that ticket won't change the results. But the process of identifying the numbers you're going to play, putting together your ticket, and deciding on the number of tickets to play has a great impact on your potential results.

A positive attitude is vital to making prudent decisions and maximizing your potential before those tickets are even chosen. Like anything else, say football or basketball, without preparation, even the best of teams would be somewhere between lousy and good—but not great. It's what happens before they ever get on the field or on the court that makes them great. They train, they prepare, they get ready to put out their best effort. If you are serious in your pursuit of jackpots, you'll need to do the same.

A negative attitude, on the other hand, works against you. It interferes with your preparation. It blocks you from identifying your best plays and numbers. It stops you from trying to achieve what you're tying to do. A negative can't-do attitude is self-defeating in anything you aspire to.

So, yes, attitude matters. Winning attitudes beget winning. "But it's just picking numbers," a naysayer might protest. "Any numbers may win." Sure, any numbers may win just like any team might win. But that attitude is for losers. Where are you putting your money—on the prepared team or on the unprepared side? With all else equal, are you betting on the team that's prepared, or the lazy competitor that moans about bad luck? It's a losing idea to throw money out there every week out of frustration or hopelessness with the attitude, "Well, I always lose, may as well keep on losing." And $10 or $20 or maybe even $50 more gets flushed down the toilet on another group of random numbers.

Stop! It's time to rethink, reenergize and go at the prospect of trying to hit winning numbers with a winning attitude. You're reading this book to change your results. Let's start with how you feel and how you're going to approach and attack lottery games.

You want an approach that gives you the feeling of power when you play. You want an approach that keeps the dream alive, makes the games more enjoyable, and gives you satisfaction in the work you put into your selection of numbers. With this kind of attitude, your wins get more intense and boost your morale. And your confidence in your strategies grows as more tickets hit and as you achieve more near misses.

And maybe, just maybe, that long shot might hit. And then *everything* will be different.

But it starts with a good attitude and the determination to put some effort into your numbers. It starts with a real plan. You want to break out of the lottery funk and throw away that defeatist attitude. And that's what I'm here to do for you. *Change everything*. Think big and think *positive*. That's the first step necessary to go after lottery and lotto games.

My goal is to make you a winner.

OVERVIEW OF LOTTERY AND LOTTO GAMES

INTRODUCTION

There are many types of lottery and lotto games, varying from as few as 10 balls in a pool to as many as 75 balls. There are games where three or four balls each are chosen from a different pool of numbers, games where five or six balls are chosen from one pool of numbers, and games such as Power Ball and Mega Millions, where there are two pools of numbers, one large pool from which five white balls are drawn, and a second, smaller pool where a single ball is drawn.

The basic thread in common between all of these games is that for a single dollar or two, you can win a massive amount of money, as much as several hundred million dollars!

I'm going to show you the best way to choose potential winning numbers so that you can get your share of millions from smaller jackpots being paid, as well as a chance at winning the huge jackpot that will change your life and put you on easy street. I'll also show you how to play your chosen numbers in wheeling systems that allow you to get a broad coverage of your numbers for a minimal investment.

The goal is to win million and millions of dollars, so much that you couldn't count all your money if you did nothing else for a month. I want you to win so much money that you can't even comprehend a number that large.

Dreams are good, my friend. Let's start chasing them!

DIFFERENCES BETWEEN LOTTERY AND LOTTO

1. In lotto, numbers are drawn from only one container, while numbers in the lottery come from separate containers.

2. In lotto, there are no duplications of numbers. For example, in a 49-ball game, exactly 49 balls numbered 1 through 49 are in the container. So if the first ball drawn is 17, it cannot be drawn again since it has already been removed. And if the second ball drawn is 49, then that too cannot be drawn again in the same game. In lottery, each container has 10 balls, numbered 0 through 9, and each ball drawn could duplicate other balls already drawn in the other tubes since they are independent events. It is not unusual to see lottery games with two or more duplicate numbers. For example, a draw could be 9-9-7 or 0-5-0.

3. In lotto, the order in which balls are drawn is irrelevant to your winning results, while in a lottery, the order of balls drawn is the difference between winning and losing. For example, if the balls drawn in a six-ball lotto game are 17, 49, 2, 10, 41 and 19, you win if enough of your numbers are drawn regardless of the order in which you picked them or in which way they are displayed.

For ease of figuring, newspapers and websites often display

the numbers in ascending order. So those winning numbers might be displayed as 2, 10, 17, 19, 41, 49. Or they may be listed like this:

$$2$$
$$10$$
$$17$$
$$19$$
$$41$$
$$49$$

In a four-ball lottery, if the numbers drawn are 9-0-3-3, having the numbers reversed to 3-3-0-9 or scrambled, as in 3-0-9-3, does you no good. Only the sequence 9-0-3-3 is a winner.

If a six-ball lottery game requires at least four of the numbers to be chosen, and you have those four numbers, you have a winner, though of course you would rather have five of the six for an even bigger prize—or all six for the jackpot!

4. In lottery games, the payoffs remain consistent. Most lottery games cost just $1 to play. Winning a Pick 3 lottery typically nets $500 in prizes while a Pick 4 might bring in $5,000. These payoffs will be posted, so you know what you're getting into before you buy your ticket. On the other hand, the jackpot in lotto games varies widely and could be huge one week and even bigger the following week. You don't know what you can win until the drawing because the jackpot grows as more people buy tickets.

WHERE TO PLAY

It's easy to find a vendor of lottery or lotto tickets. Tickets are offered in an endless number of locations, typically convenience stores where customers can buy their essentials — milk, bread, and lottery tickets — as well as in other outlets such as grocery stores, liquor stores, variety stores and supermarkets.

California alone has more than 20,000 locations where players can buy lottery tickets and hope to score their dreams. New York boasts 16,500+ outlets, and Florida offers another 13,000.

Theoretically, it makes no difference where you buy your tickets, but if you feel luckier in one location than another, go with your gut. No reason not to.

OVERVIEW OF THE GAMES

INSTANT GAMES

Since you can't choose your own numbers and are given tickets with predetermined printed numbers, you can't use any of the winning methods in this book when you play instant games. Basically, you either win or lose depending on the number that gets revealed when you scratch off the covering.

If you're going to play these instant scratch-off types of tickets, your best strategy is to go for prizes that make it worthwhile. If they're going to bleed you dry dollar by dollar, then you at least want a chance at winning something that will make a difference. After all, that's why you're playing these games in the first place, right? Everyone has their own baseline for what will make a difference in their lives, but it seems to me that going for a prize of at least $10,000 is a worthy enough floor. If the instant games don't offer that kind of prize, you might consider passing on playing them.

THREE-BALL AND FOUR-BALL LOTTERY

1. Basic Game

Three-ball and four-ball lotteries are a centerpiece in many players' daily or weekly lottery routine. These games are offered throughout the country in almost all states and are extremely popular. They offer fast results, big prizes, and keep players consistently involved so that they can get their fix.

There are three separate containers in three-ball lottery games and four separate containers in four-ball lottery games, with each container filled with 10 balls numbered 0 through 9. A ball will be drawn from each container, in order, until all the balls for the game have been drawn; that is, three-balls in the three-ball game and four-balls in the four-ball game. Thus, you might see the numbers 0-9-8 drawn in a three-ball game, and 7-0-7-3 drawn in a four-ball game.

The winning tickets would match these numbers: 0-9-8 and 7-0-7-3 in the three-ball and four-ball games, respectively. If your three-ball ticket read 0-9-8, you would be a winner. If your ticket read 9-8-0, however, it would not be a winner—it would be a loser, even though you held the correct three digits. In traditional lottery games, the order in which numbers are drawn counts for everything because payouts are not for three correctly chosen numbers in a random sequence, they are for three correctly chosen numbers *in the exact order* in which they were drawn.

For another example, if the numbers drawn are 5-7-3 in that order, and you chose those three numbers but in a different order, 3-5-7, you have as equal a loser as you would've had if your ticket had read 8-6-9, none of which numbers were picked. The winning combination must match the order chosen and only 5-7-3 in the example above, and 0-9-8 in the earlier example, would be winning combinations.

Note that in our earlier four-ball draw of 7-0-7-3, the number 7 was repeated twice in the drawing. In lottery that is possible because each number is drawn from a different container with balls numbered 0 through 9. It could even be drawn three times, or four times in a four-ball game, as in 7-7-7-7. In lotto games, however, that is not possible since there are no duplicate numbers in the bins. Once a 7 is drawn, another 7 cannot be pulled for that drawing. The following day it could, but not today. The other five balls would comprise some combination of the remaining numbers in the bin.

2. Enhanced Three-Ball and Four-Ball Lottery Games

In the last bunch of years, as a way to attract more money into the game, three-ball and four-ball lotteries have added more ways to win. Borrowing from the popularity of horseracing bets, additional plays allow you to win in more ways than simply picking the winning number in the *exact order* drawn, known as a **straight bet**. In states offering these options, now you can also *box* your numbers, known as a **box bet**, and have the three numbers appear in any order. Or you can play a **straight/box bet**, where you win if the ticket comes in exactly as you picked or if it comes in any order, which is actually a two-ticket play. Or you can play a **combination bet**, which is actually a six-ticket bet since you are playing all six combinations possible in the three-ball game.

SIX-BALL LOTTO GAMES

The six-ball lotto games generate a tremendous amount of excitement among players. Huge $100 million jackpots and multi-hundred million dollar jackpots create a groundswell of play from not just regular players but also from occasional and new players who can't wait to get their shot at a payday that is the stuff that dreams are made of.

There are many variations of six-ball games, but they all work more or less the same way. The typical six-ball lotto game costs $1 to play and features a total pool of 49 balls, numbered 1-49, from which six balls will be chosen. The numbers on those six balls will be the winning combination. For example, if the numbers drawn are 12-15-22-28-44-47, the life of the player who picked those numbers will never be the same again. Having a ticket with all six winning numbers wins the jackpot! Smaller cash prizes will be awarded to tickets that contain five of the six drawn numbers, and also to tickets with three and four winning numbers. Tickets with just one or two of the drawn numbers, or no drawn numbers, win nothing. The fewer the numbers matched, the easier it is to hit and the more small winners there are. The more numbers you hit the greater the payout with the granddaddy, of course, being all six numbers and a huge jackpot.

While the six-ball lotto games with 49 total balls—called the **6/49 game**—are very popular, you will also find games with balls drawn from a larger pool. For example, a **6/51 game** will have a pool of 51 numbers from which the six winning balls will be drawn, and there is even a **6/54 game**. There are also games with fewer total balls in the pool, such as 6/42, 6/46 and 6/47. Each state follows its own regulations for offering lotto games and has its own offerings.

Most six-ball lotto games are held biweekly, with drawings typically on Wednesday and Saturday nights. If there are multiple winners for the jackpot, that is, if two or more players correctly pick all six numbers, the jackpot is split among them. If there are no winners, the jackpot rolls over to the next drawing, greatly increasing the following week's pool and making the game that much more exciting. If enough weeks go by without a winner, the potential jackpot starts making national news and everybody wants to get in on the act.

The amount of money you can win is entirely dependent on the total prize pool for that week, that is, the total number of tickets sold. Lotto is a **pari-mutuel game**, meaning that the total amount bet, less money taken by the government for its fees and costs, is available for the prize pool. The greater the number of tickets sold the greater the jackpot.

FIVE-BALL LOTTO GAMES (LITTLE LOTTO)

There are also **five-ball lotto games**, also known as **Little Lottos**, which draw from smaller pools of numbers, such as 36 or 39, and pick only five balls. The game works the same as the six-ball version, except that it is easier to win since only five balls must be hit. Little Lotto games are played more frequently, often six or seven days a week, than the six-ball game. Fewer tickets are sold for the more frequent five-ball games, so the prizes are much smaller amounts.

MULTI-STATE (DUAL-POOL) LOTTERY GAMES

The **multi-state games** feature balls drawn from two separate drums. They accumulate massive jackpots that make players drool for astronomically large prizes. As the windfall grows into the high tens of millions—and sometimes hundreds of millions—regular players and even casual observers begin buying tickets like crazy, hoping to be the lucky individual that pulls down the miracle.

Mega-Millions and Powerball, the two largest multi-state lottery games, get the most attention because they accumulate the largest jackpots. Both Mega Millions and Powerball have had multiple jackpots in excess of *one-half billion dollars*—an insane amount of money—and tons more in the hundreds of millions of dollars. The increase in price of the Powerball ticket to $2 and the lengthening in odds for Mega Millions in the early 2010s have accounted for the huge increase in jackpots compared to prior years.

Powerball is played in more than 40 states, plus Washington D.C., Puerto Rico and the U.S. Virgin Islands. Every Wednesday and Saturday night at 10:59 pm Eastern Standard Time, five balls are drawn out of a drum with 69 white balls and one ball is drawn out of a drum with 26 red balls. The winner or winners of the jackpot (won by correctly picking the five white balls and the one red Powerball) can choose to get 30 payouts over 29 years (the first payment occurs immediately) or a one-time payment of the entire jackpot. The second prize (won by correctly picking the five white balls) is $1,000,000 and is paid out in one lump sum.

Mega Millions is also played in more than 40 states, plus Washington D.C. and the U.S. Virgin Islands. Drawings are held every Tuesday and Friday at 11:00 pm Eastern Standard Time. Like Powerball, there are two pools of balls. One pool contains 75 white balls, out of which five balls are drawn, and a second pool, containing 15 gold balls, from which one ball is drawn. The jackpot starts at $15 million and grows by a minimum of $5 million each time it is not hit. Winners can take the jackpot in one lump sum (equal to all the cash in the Mega Millions jackpot pool) or take the money in 30 payments, one upon winning, and one each over the next 29 years. The second prize, as in Powerball, is $1,000,000. It costs $1 to play Mega Millions.

There are other popular multi-state games, including Hot Lotto, Lucky for Life, Wild Card 2, 2by2, MegaHits and Tri-State Megabucks Plus.

Multi-state games are offered in all U.S. states that offer lottery and lotto games; however, some are regional in nature, such as Tri-State Megabucks Plus, which is played only in Vermont, New Hampshire and Maine.

Six states ban lottery-type games: Nevada, Utah, Mississippi, Alabama, Alaska and Hawaii.

5

THE THEORY OF BEATING THE LOTTERY

This chapter is devoted to giving you a brief sense of what we're trying to do with our strategies, as well as providing the realities of playing lottery and lotto games. I touch on a just a brief amount of math to illustrate a few points, but not too much—I promise!

FACTS AND FLIPS VERSUS MATH

Lottery and lotto are negative expectation games. What that means is that in the long run, you are playing at a mathematical disadvantage, and the odds are that the house will win. I must be clear with you on that. No matter what you do, it is likely that you will lose money playing the lottery or lotto, in the short run and in the long run. That is a simple, straightforward fact.

But despite the many losers, some people are winners—and very big winners at that. Why them? What makes these players the fortunate ones who take home the millions and hundreds of millions of dollars?

There is no easy answer. In fact, the answer is extremely difficult to approach. But I will dance around the edges in the following discussion, which will give you some way of understanding how math and the unpredictable both intersect and remain foreign to one another.

People like to feel that they can influence their destiny, that their decisions can position them to do better in life, as well as in gambling. With many things that supposition is entirely true, though it doesn't always work out in an expected or favorable manner. People feel the same way about lottery and lotto games. They want to influence their results by picking better numbers. Rather than stumbling blindly through these games, players want a feeling of control. They watch drawings and observe patterns. Real patterns. Groups of numbers that repeat more often than others over specified periods of time, with an individual number or two perhaps greatly outperforming that group of stars. And some numbers just never seem to get drawn.

Had you played the good numbers, the stars and the superstars, and shunned the bad ones over that period of time, you would have won money. Perhaps even a lot of money.

Looking forward, you think that maybe that run of numbers is over and you feel that it's time to play the cold numbers because their time is due, or you might say, overdue. If you flip coins, it wouldn't be unusual to catch three heads in a row, or even four. You would not be shocked by that result at all. If you were betting on the heads, you'd be as happy as pie, but if you were on the other side of the proposition, you would curse your bad luck. An innocent observer watching the coin flips wouldn't think much about the occurrence because, as I pointed out above, it is not a shocking set of circumstances. If you flipped a coin right now, the odds for heads to come up three times in succession would be 7 to 1 against, and four times in succession would be 15 to 1 against. Longer odds than you might guess at first thought, but how many times have you seen 50-50 propositions go on even longer runs that that?

But you also think that over the long run, heads will come up about half the time, that is 50% of the time, and tails the other 50% of the time. The expectation would be that over time, the "long run," one event would come up about as much as the other event.

There is a subtle flaw in that argument, but if you subscribed to that statement, you would be absolutely correct. Over 1,000 flips—and certainly over 10,000 flips—of that coin, even given a start where the first four flips were heads, the end result of a larger number of coin flips would be awfully close to 50% heads and 50% tails on a percentage basis. You would observe these results and reasonably and accurately say that the coin flip was a 50-50 proposition.

The flaw?

While the percentages would be very close to 50-50 in the coin flip, it is highly unlikely that the actual results would be *exactly* 5,000 heads and 5,000 tails They would be "reasonably" close, close enough that you could fairly say that the results were *about* 50-50 (since it might be 50.38% heads and 49.62% tails). Since we are going to round off decimal points in a normal conversation, and perhaps even in a mathematical discourse (with the understanding that we were not talking about *exactly* 50-50), 50-50 might be the mathematical statement expressed. In fact, if you ran that 10,000-flip trial five times, it is very unlikely that even one of the trials would be exactly 5,000 heads and 5,000 tails. Add up the five trials together, a total of 50,000 flips, and you would again approximate 50-50, probably more so than the individual trial that brought us to 50.38%-49.62%.

But let me not get too deep into the math and lose you here, or lose the point, which is what you can mathematically expect or practically expect from random occurrences.

Let's come back to the first four flips of that coin, all of which were heads. If we are working with a normal coin that is not gaffed or weighted such that the coin flip wasn't random and the flip wasn't influenced by a mechanic (a person who could influence the results through sleight of hand), then we're contemplating what might occur on the fifth flip so that we might bet on it. Several thoughts might occur. First, heads are *hot* and that's where our best bet might be. We thought this on the third flip of heads and, sure enough, another head was flipped. Heads are hot and on a streak. That is undeniable, no matter what you believe in.

We might take the contrary position. Tails are *due*.

Mathematically, we know that the odds of four flips in a row coming up heads are 15 to 1 against, and for five times in a row, those odds skyrocket to 31 to 1 against. We also know that in the long run, heads and tails will each come up around 50% of the time, so tails are overdue. But the heads bettor will say that you can't ignore streaks, math be damned. The tails bettor had those thoughts on the third flip of heads and was wrong, and he was wrong on the fourth. The heads bettor says he will be wrong again.

Another idea is creeping into your consciousness, an idea that is backed by what you have seen on the first four flips: There is a bias in the coin, or in the process of flipping that coin, which makes the flip more likely to be heads.

Mathematically, in a coin flip, past results don't affect the chances of future flips landing heads or tails, but that fact won't dissuade people from observing trends, patterns, hot numbers and omissions, and betting accordingly. There *was* a reason four heads in a row came up, whether you can discern that reason or not, because the fact remains: Four heads in a row were flipped.

While lottery and lotto players are not mathematicians, they are keen observers of past results and they can clearly see which numbers are repeating more often than others, and which are repeating less often. Players who look for any way they can to gain an edge cannot ignore patterns of numbers and winners in prior results. Talk all you want about math and expectations and percentages, the numbers that were drawn are as clear as daylight. Anyone can see that some numbers have performed better than other numbers, and some worse.

And again, there was a reason for that.

For this latter group of people, the observers that say you cannot ignore what you see with your own eyes, that the results are real—which indeed they are if they have occurred—a wealth of strategies is available to beat the lottery and lotto games.

UNDERSTANDING BIAS

Not everything is constructed perfectly. Variances in material as it gets pulled into the construction process, construction methods, weather or atmospheric conditions as items are produced (even occurring on a minute by minute basis), and a host of other variables interweave so that no two items are exactly the same—not two pencils, not two pieces of wood, not two slabs of concrete, not even two pieces of plastic. To the eye, the items may to be perfect replicas of one another, but if you examine them under a microscope, imperfections get revealed.

This holds equally true with balls manufactured for the lottery. It is impossible to make two balls exactly alike. To the eye, again, that may be the case. But if you pulled out a microscope or dissected the ball under that microscope, you would find different surface areas and varying densities in the material used to make the ball. There would be irregularities and micro-level imperfections. Are they enough to make a difference? Probably. But the real question is: Are they imperfect enough to alter the expected results in a given number of events?

In other words, have they created a *bias*?

Maybe.

When mechanical devices are involved, any imperfection causes what is called a **bias**, a tendency of certain events to occur at a greater or lesser frequency than pure randomness would suggest because of physical irregularities. The physical balls used in lotteries are not perfect, though the manufacturers work hard to get them as close as possible. Every ball manufactured is different from every other, and the slightest imperfection or difference affects its chances of being selected. For example, the amount of paint being affixed to the ball will affect the way it spins and moves. We're not just describing the density of the ink as it lays on the ball, which will differ from ball to ball, we're describing the numbers themselves. A cursory observation tells us that the number 37 has more ink than the number 7.

How will that affect the results? It is almost impossible to predict, but through observation, you can certainly see the results and chart them.

There will also be slight variances in the weight of one ball compared to another—though a normal scale may not be able to detect the difference (you would likely need a highly sensitive scale that weighed items in micro measurements)—the density in parts of the ball, and even the smoothness and pitting of the surface, among other variables.

In any game where physical properties are involved, like lottery drawings or even roulette, bias is a factor that must be considered. You don't need to be able to identify the actual bias because, even if you did, you likely wouldn't be able to predict how it would affect results. You just need to identify patterns that emerge through actual events. Some incredible hauls have been made at roulette by observant players who clocked wheels and identified biases, making a fortune betting the biased numbers—at least until the casinos wised up that something was wrong and changed the equipment.

So then, you might ask, how you would discover a bias? The short answer is pretty much the same way that you would discover hot numbers. We'll get to the long answer later when we learn how to chart prior draws. The key answer in either case—a bias or a hot number—is to identify exactly what patterns have emerged in a recent history of drawings.

The results will be plain as day.

GETTING YOUR HANDS DIRTY

Now that we've gotten some of the basics out of the way, let's get into the meat, starting with a strategy overview so that you will have a sense of how you're going to attack the game with directed strategies.

Your goal, of course, is to choose a ticket that will make you rich beyond belief.

SECTION II

TOOLS, ANALYSES, STRATEGIES

6

STRATEGY OVERVIEW

The heart of all lottery systems and strategies relies on gathering a past history of winning numbers and isolating patterns that have shown a prevalence to occur, or not to occur, and then using that information to predict future results. We discussed the theory of beating lottery and lotto in the previous chapter, *The Theory of Beating the Lottery*.

There are different approaches to deciphering and exploiting past results, but the two main ones basically divide along the lines of betting numbers that have shown a higher than average frequency of occurrence or the opposite, betting numbers that have not occurred and are "overdue." It is almost like pass and don't pass in craps, or red and black in roulette. Players on each side of the divide take contrary positions.

There are other workable approaches as well that either riff off these two main lines, identify groups of balls that were drawn (or not drawn) together, or that follow unorthodox patterns that don't fit into two classifications.

The key to all our strategies and the basis of everything you will do relies on accurately charting a history of previous winning numbers. There are various levels of complexities and, as we discussed above, different approaches to identifying prior winning numbers that you will use as the basis for making tickets.

I have divided the strategies you will use into three broad categories: Level I Strategies, Level II Strategies, and Level III Strategies.

SIMPLIFIED BLUEPRINT FOR PICKING NUMBERS

The chart below is an oversimplification of my approach to picking numbers, but for our purposes now, it will do to get the conversation going. I'll go into greater detail as we move through the book

---

SIMPLIFIED BLUEPRINT FOR PICKING NUMBERS

---

1. Use your tools to determine a pattern.
2. Analyze the patterns and determine the various ways to take advantage of them.
3. Use specially designed wheels to bet your numbers, ones that give you a greatly increased probability of winning should your chosen numbers be drawn.

LEVEL I, LEVEL II & LEVEL III STRATEGIES

Here is a brief overview of the three classes of strategies for beating lottery and lotto games:

LEVEL I STRATEGIES

Level I Strategies, or the **Core Strategies**, are the powerful everyday strategies you will use to beat lottery and lotto games. These core strategies are the rice-and-beans approach that forms the backbone of all the strategies you will use. The

Level II and Level III strategies build upon the groundwork laid by Level I analysis.

LEVEL II STRATEGIES

Level II Strategies identify the most important of our chosen numbers—or introduce numbers from outside that group—and play these numbers more aggressively than the other chosen numbers in the pool. With Level II strategies, you use advanced analyses to identify a special number or numbers and elevate them to a higher status.

LEVEL III STRATEGIES

Level III Strategies use Level I core strategies and Level II key numbers as centerpieces to form straightforward or intricate strategies designed to beat lottery and lotto games. There are also very advanced Level III strategies, called **Exotics**, that are known and used by only an elite few.

ADVANTAGES OF PLAYING LOTTERY AND LOTTO GAMES COMPARED TO CASINO GAMES

1. Unlike card games such as blackjack or poker, you choose your own numbers to play.

2. You can bet as little as you like or as much as you like. No one can tell you how much to bet or how many tickets to play. It's your decision.

3. Unlike many casino games, you can take advantage of your knowledge of past numbers drawn to choose future numbers.

These are the strategies you will use to beat the lottery: Level I, Level II and Level III strategies. In laymen terms, they are the Core Strategies, the Keys and the Advanced Strategies.

A FEW IMPORTANT CONCEPTS AND TERMS

CHOSEN NUMBERS

The main function of the Level I strategies and analyses is to identify the numbers that give you the best chance to win. These numbers are called **chosen numbers**; that is, the numbers you choose to play on your tickets. For example, let's say you identify 12 numbers that you like—that is, 12 chosen numbers. If you play every one of them in every combination, you would spend a fortune in tickets trying to catch a six-ball lotto jackpot.

To be economical and not play recklessly or worse, go broke, you would choose a reasonable number of combinations of the numbers to play tickets—according to your budget—but not all of them. I will cover how to do this in the *Wheeling Strategy* chapter, but for now, the concept to understand is why you will choose certain numbers to play on tickets and avoid others.

That brings us to the next concept.

CONFIDENCE LEVEL

One important concept to understand, and which I will refer to throughout the strategies, is called *confidence level*. The meaning is pretty much the same as it sounds. A **confidence level** represents your level of confidence in a number. As a result, you'll play higher confidence numbers in your pool of chosen numbers more heavily, and ones with a lesser confidence less heavily. Don't get me wrong. You want to play all your chosen numbers—these are your highest performing numbers—but some of these chosen numbers are more important than other ones. And you'll treat them that way. This concept of a confidence level is at the heart of the Level II strategies and will be covered in the Level II Strategies: Key Numbers chapter.

REGRESSION ANALYSIS

Regression analysis is an analysis over a specified number of prior lottery or lotto drawings (called a **regression level**). For example, you could run a regression analysis of 25 games or. 100 games.

You may decide, for instance, to study patterns and trends by taking a regression analysis of 50 games, 100 games or 250 games, depending on your philosophical approach or the dictates of the particular strategy you're playing. Various strategies require deep levels of regression while others require as few as five or ten drawings.

In Level III strategies, regression analysis takes on a more prominent role. Many Level III strategies call for particular regression levels, sometimes combining different penetration depths to identify streaks and patterns. For example, a Level III play may ask for a 100-game analysis to pick up eight numbers, along with a 10-game analysis to identify other chosen numbers.

When you run a regression analysis with a particular strategy, you are given instructions on the optimal number of games to chart. Some strategies may ask for deep penetration and other strategies may concentrate on shallow penetration, saying that only the very latest data are relevant.

Here is terminology you should be conversant with for regression levels.

REGRESSION LEVEL TERMINOLOGY

Term	Regression Level
Burst	10 Games or Less
Run it Short	11-50 Games
Run it Soft	51-99 Games
Run it Solid	100-149 Games
Run it Long	150+ Games

The decision to chart a burst, run it short, or run it long—or anything in between—is dependent on philosophical goals or particular strategy dictates. When playing particular strategies that don't have built-in regression requirements, it is often prudent to run it solid, maybe a 100-game regression level, to ensure you have enough of a history to get stable results. Of course, when you get to certain Level III strategies, you will use a range of regression levels depending upon the depth being targeted. But for now, running it solid is the recommended default unless otherwise determined.

SUMMING UP

We've given you an overview of the Level I, Level II and Level III strategies and have introduced you to the important concepts of chosen numbers and confidence level. With that in our ammunition box, let's add more weapons to our arsenal and move on to the foundation of our winning approach.

7

LEVEL I PLAY: THE CORE STRATEGIES

In this section we'll present an overview of the Level I strategies, the backbone of our attack in the lottery and lotto games. These are the **core strategies,** powerful everyday strategies you will use to beat lotto and lottery games—the foundation of your entire winning approach. Once you fully understand the Level I core strategies and are conversant with how to use them, you will be able to add a more sophisticated approach—if it suits your overall approach—by adding Level II and then, Level III strategies.

But first, you must fully understand and be able to use the material covered in this chapter, the powerful core strategies that are the heart and soul of our approach.

In a nutshell, the core strategies seek to identify the most favorable numbers for the analyses you will use—these are your chosen numbers. This is the pool of numbers that will comprise the heart of your winning tickets.

Let's dig deeper and see how you do that.

POSITIONAL ANALYSIS (LOTTERY)

In lottery games, a drawing such as 3-8-0 is different than one with the same numbers but in a different order, such as 0-3-8. Same three numbers, but a distinctly different combination because order of draw is important in three-ball lottery games, as well as in four-ball lottery games.

When you chart numbers in lottery games, you don't blindly list the digits drawn. It would take close to 1,000 daily drawings in three-ball lottery games—combinations of 0-0-0 all the way to 9-9-9—if each combination were to be drawn exactly once before a repeated combination occurred. That's almost three years! In reality many combinations would repeat two times, three times and even more before other numbers occurred on even a single occasion. You would wait more than three years of daily drawings before every single combination occurred at least once. That wouldn't give you much to work with and you couldn't form a useful strategy with a combination pool that vast. You'd never get anywhere.

More importantly, charting numbers as an individual group of three numbers would make no sense because each digit in a three-ball lottery is drawn from its own pool and is independent of the other digits being drawn. So, obviously, that fruitless path is negated.

Instead, you track each combination by its individual digits by running a *positional analysis*. **Positional analysis** is the science of charting and statistically identifying and analyzing balls by position from a specified number of previous games in which each ball gets drawn from a different bin, such as happens in three-ball and four-ball lottery games. Your analysis will track the results of each ball drawn and parse the information so that you can run further analyses from this data, such as numbers that were most frequently drawn and ones that were least frequently drawn.

HOW TO MAKE POSITIONAL ANALYSIS CHARTS

Using our earlier example of the three-ball draw, you wouldn't track the number 380 as a whole, but rather, individually, by position. You would track the individual digits 3-8-0 in this example. The dashes are used to separate the drawn numbers. The result 3-8-0 signifies that the 3-ball was drawn from the first pool, the 8-ball from the second pool, and the 0-ball from the third pool.

The first 10 drawings, were as follows: 3-8-0, 5-1-5, 1-0-3, 0-8-2, 5-1-2, 7-7-3, 0-2-9, 9-6-6, 6-3-1, 8-0-2. You separate the number of each ball drawn by a dash to indicate its standing as an individual number.

You chart the information by column to show that the balls were drawn from their own individual bins. Your positional analysis will parse each number into its own column and tally the results so that you can examine each bin on its own merits.

To properly track these numbers, you create a worksheet with three columns, one for each number drawn.

First, let's show a blank worksheet that you could use as a template to chart results from three-ball lottery, games and then a worksheet reflecting 10 drawings. We're indicating each number by position by marking the corresponding area in the matrix with a dot.

POSITIONAL ANALYSIS
Blank Worksheet

Balls	Position 1	Position 2	Position 3
0			
1			
2			
3			
4			
5			
6			
7			
8			
9			

POSITIONAL ANALYSIS
10 Games Charted

Balls	Position 1	Position 2	Position 3
0	••	••	•
1	•	••	•
2		•	•••
3	•	•	••
4			
5	••		•
6	•	•	•
7	•	•	
8	•	••	
9	•		•

You'll put these results into a *Positional Drawing History*. A **Positional Drawing History** shows the date of drawing and the balls selected for each drawing, by position, over a specified number of lottery drawings. In this case, we're showing a three-ball lottery game, hence, in addition to the column showing the date of the drawing, there is a column for each of the three balls.

POSITIONAL DRAWING HISTORY
Three-Ball Lottery / 10 Drawings

Date	Position		
	1	**2**	**3**
1/3	3	8	0
1/4	5	1	5
1/5	1	0	3
1/6	0	8	2
1/7	5	1	2
1/8	7	7	3
1/9	0	2	9
1/10	9	6	6
1/11	6	3	1
1/12	8	0	2

Each horizontal row represents a three-ball drawing on the date indicated, and the columns chart the ball drawn in each of the three positions. Position 1 shows the first ball drawn, Position 2 shows the second ball drawn, and Position 3 shows the third and last ball drawn.

Let's now look at a Positional Drawing History showing a four-ball lottery game so that you can see what it looks like. It is exactly the same as the three-ball Positional Drawing History chart except that there is an additional column to chart the fourth ball.

POSITIONAL DRAWING HISTORY
Four-Ball Lottery / 10 Drawings

Date	Position 1	2	3	4
8/1	8	0	3	3
8/2	1	0	5	2
8/3	9	7	2	8
8/4	4	5	4	2
8/5	6	8	6	1
8/6	1	3	0	8
8/7	4	9	0	1
8/8	8	3	3	4
8/9	9	1	8	8
8/10	9	8	2	2

Each horizontal row represents a four-ball drawing on the date indicated, and the columns chart the ball drawn in each of the four positions. Position 1 shows the first ball drawn, Position 2 shows the second ball drawn, Position 3 shows the third ball drawn, and Position 4 shows the fourth and last ball drawn.

The Positional Drawing History organizes the drawings in an easy-to-see format so you can zoom right in on any drawing and immediately see the results, or scan up and down columns to track patterns. But to understand the frequency of occurrence in a large number of drawings, or even in a short range, you need a chart set up for this purpose. For that, you need a *Positional Analysis Raw Chart*.

A **Positional Analysis Raw Chart** keeps track of the frequency of drawings for each digit in a lottery over a specified regression level.

In the example below, we're charting only 10 games. Each time a ball is drawn, you mark a dot in the appropriate area in the matrix. If the drawing was 8-3-0-4, you would put a dot in the first column by the number 8, a dot in the second column by the number 6, a dot in the third column by the number 0, and a dot in the fourth column by the number 4.

We did this for 10 drawings and these were the results we got.

	1	2	3	4
0		••	••	
1	••	•		••
2			••	•••
3		••	••	•
4	••		•	•
5		•	•	
6	•		•	
7		•		
8	••	••	•	•••
9	•••	•		

POSITIONAL ANALYSIS RAW CHART
Four-Ball Lottery / 10 Drawings

In this small sample, you start to see patterns emerging. Some numbers in the first column were drawn more often than others, and some less. You'll observe similar patterns, but different number results, in columns 2, 3 and 4. You'll also see numbers didn't hit at all.

The Positional Analysis Raw Chart is a worksheet of raw data for lottery games. But to make this information easier to use, you convert the dots into numbers. Now, at a glance, you can easily see the best performers. This chart, which refines the data from the dots in a Positional Analysis Raw Chart into numbers is called a **Positional Analysis Refined Chart**.

Analyzing charts in number form, as opposed to dots, is much easier to do.

POSITIONAL ANALYSIS REFINED CHART
Four-Ball Lottery / 10 Drawings

	1	2	3	4
0		2	2	
1	2	1		2
2			2	3
3		2	2	1
4	2		1	1
5		1	1	
6	1		1	
7		1		
8	2	2	1	3
9	3	1		

This chart represents a small history of just 10 games. Let's say you're tracking 100 games. It might look like this:

POSITIONAL ANALYSIS REFINED CHART
Four-Ball Lottery / 100 Drawings

	1	2	3	4
0	7	17	14	8
1	13	11	4	12
2	5	10	15	14
3	14	7	11	7
4	9	11	7	13
5	6	8	8	11
6	8	8	7	11
7	10	11	12	7
8	15	12	11	8
9	13	5	11	9

At a glance, you can see how numbers have performed over a 100 game regression. However, to make this information more useful, you need to refine the information. That is, you need to parse and analyze the data for specific patterns.

The most important of these analyses are a Best Number Analysis and an Overdue Number Analysis. Let's look at them now.

BEST NUMBER ANALYSIS

A **Best Number Analysis** is a handy tool that organizes the numbers, by position, from the results of the Positional Analysis Refined Chart with the specific purpose of identifying numbers that have been the most frequently drawn over a specified number of games. It takes the raw information and shows the frequency of occurrence in order and by position, so that you can easily see the number of times each ball was drawn starting with the top performing number on the first line. For example, you might run a Best Number Analysis with a regression level of 35 games, or perhaps 100 games, or even 250 games.

You are analyzing the best (hot) numbers in this case and showing just the top three performing balls. A bigger chart might display the best 10 numbers or even the full range of all possible numbers, but since you are only looking for the top three performing numbers right now, only those results are shown. If you were running a more aggressive set of tickets, you would display the top five results, or even more.

We're building information, albeit a small sample at this point. For this chart to have greater significance, you'll need a longer history. But first, let's see where we are right now for the previous 10 games, and take notice of the early tendencies as we begin to form our winning ticket combinations.

BEST NUMBER ANALYSIS
Four-Ball Lottery / 10 Drawings

Position 1		Position 2		Position 3		Position 4		
#	Frq	#	Frq	#	Frq	#	Frq	Best Numbers
9	3	0	2	0	2	8	3	Most Draws
1	2	8	2	3	2	1	2	Second Most
8	2	3	2	-	-	2	2	Third Most

"#" is the number drawn; shown in bold type.
"Frq" is the frequency of occurrence shown in normal (non-bold) type.
"Best Numbers" displays the balls most frequently drawn, in order.
"Position 1" indicates the first ball drawn, "Position 2" the second ball drawn, and so on.
The final column notes the order of appearance. That is, the most occurrences (best or hottest numbers), then the second, third and fourth most occurrences, in order.

I have shown examples of a 10-game regression for ease of explanation. Depending on the strategy you employ to attack past history, you might do regression levels of 25 games, 100 games or even as high as 250 games or more. With larger sample sizes, there would be fewer ties and more distinct results. Following are the top results from the 100-game drawing we showed earlier, organized into a Best Number Analysis.

BEST NUMBER ANALYSIS
Four-Ball Lottery / 100 Drawings

Position 1		Position 2		Position 3		Position 4		
#	**Frq**	**#**	**Frq**	**#**	**Frq**	**#**	**Frq**	**Best Numbers**
8	15	0	17	2	15	2	14	Most Draws
3	14	8	12	0	14	4	13	Second Most
1	13	-	-	7	12	1	12	Third Most
9	13	-	-	-	-	-	-	Fourth Most

These are your hottest numbers, by position, over the 100-game drawing sampled. For Position 2, I omitted the third most frequently drawn number because there were actually three ties in that position. In Position 1 I showed the tie for the fourth hottest number.

OVERDUE NUMBER ANALYSIS (COLD NUMBERS)

An **Overdue Number Analysis** refines data from Frequency Analysis or Positional Analysis charts by organizing and identifying **overdue numbers**—numbers that have been the least frequently drawn over a specified number of games—and displaying them in order of least frequently drawn to most frequently drawn—exactly the opposite of the Best Number Analysis.

You rely on the same charts you used to identify the hot numbers except that, in this particular case, you are going to extract the cold numbers.

An Overdue Number Analysis is counterintuitive to players who subscribe to the theory that you should play the numbers that get drawn more frequently than others. Some players like to go against the grain (and trends) for their profits, like wrong bettors (don't pass and don't come) in craps, and underdog bettors in sports. Some of these players have enjoyed great success going against the flow.

We recreate our Positional Drawing History chart from the earlier ten-game drawing.

POSITIONAL DRAWING HISTORY
Four-Ball Lottery / 10 Drawings

Date	Position 1	2	3	4
8/1	8	0	3	3
8/2	1	0	5	2
8/3	9	7	2	8
8/4	4	5	4	2
8/5	6	8	6	1
8/6	1	3	0	8
8/7	4	9	0	1
8/8	8	3	3	4
8/9	9	1	8	8
8/10	9	8	7	9

You rearrange the numbers so that they are in order from fewest times drawn to most times drawn.

OVERDUE NUMBER ANALYSIS
Four-Ball Lottery / 10 Drawings

Position 1		Position 2		Position 3		Position 4		
#	**Frq**	**#**	**Frq**	**#**	**Frq**	**#**	**Frq**	**Overdue #s**
0	0	**2**	0	**1**	0	**0**	0	Fewest Draws
2	0	**4**	0	**9**	0	**5**	0	Second Fewest
3	0	**6**	-	-	-	**6**	0	Third Fewest
5	0	-	-	-	-	**7**	0	Fourth Fewest
7	0	-	-	-	-	-	-	

"#" is the number drawn shown in bold type.

"Frq" is the frequency of occurrence shown in normal (non-bold) type.

"Overdue Numbers" displays the balls least frequently drawn, in order.

"Position 1" indicates the first ball drawn, "Position 2" the second ball drawn, and so on.

The final column notes the order of appearance. That is, the fewest occurrences (overdue or cold numbers), then the second, third and fourth least occurrences, in order.

In the overdue numbers section, you see that Position 1 has five numbers that haven't been drawn a single time, the 0, 2, 3, 5 and 7. Position 2 has three numbers that haven't been drawn, the 2, 4 and 6. Position 3 has two numbers, 1 and 9, that haven't been drawn, and Position 4 has four numbers that haven't been drawn, the 0, 5, 6 and 7.

This sample size is so small that you have a lot of numbers that haven't yet had much of a chance to get drawn, showing that a 10-game Overdue Number Analysis in lottery is not large enough to get significant results for playing cold numbers.

In this 10-game analysis, there are 14 numbers that haven't been drawn on a single occasion in their position.

Clearly, you need more history and a greater distinction of numbers to get a higher confidence level for choosing over-due numbers and forming tickets. Unless you are running s specialized short-term regression play as part of an advanced Level III strategy, I would recommend a regression level of at least 25 or 50 games.

Let's show an Overdue Number Analysis for a 100-game drawing. We'll use the earlier results from the Best Number Analysis, though of course, we flip the results. Here is the Positional Analysis Refined Chart that we extracted the data from.

POSITIONAL ANALYSIS REFINED CHART
4-Ball Lottery / 100 Drawings

	1	2	3	4
0	7	17	14	8
1	13	11	4	12
2	5	10	15	14
3	14	7	11	7
4	9	11	7	13
5	6	8	8	11
6	8	8	7	11
7	10	11	12	7
8	15	12	11	8
9	13	5	11	9

Following are the top results from the 100-game drawing we showed earlier, organized into an Overdue Number Analysis.

OVERDUE NUMBER ANALYSIS
4-Ball Lottery / 100 Drawings

Position 1		Position 2		Position 3		Position 4		
#	Frq	#	Frq	#	Frq	#	Frq	Overdue #s
2	5	9	5	1	4	3	7	Fewest Draws
5	6	3	7	4	7	7	7	Second Fewest
0	8	5	8	6	7	0	8	Third Fewest
-	-	6	8	-	-	8	8	Fourth Fewest

These are your most overdue numbers, by position, over the 100-game drawing sampled. In Positions 2 and 4, I showed the tie for the fourth-most overdue numbers.

SUMMING UP

Let me sum up the process of identifying overdue numbers:

1. Start With a Positional Drawing History
2. Create a Positional Analysis Raw Chart
3. Create a Positional Analysis Refined Chart
4. Extract an Overdue Number Analysis Chart

Now you have your most overdue numbers in an easy-to-use format.

FREQUENCY ANALYSIS (LOTTO)

The foundation of all your winning strategies in lotto games is the powerful *frequency analysis* tool. **Frequency analysis** is the science of charting and statistically analyzing the winning balls in lotto games from a specified number of previous drawings. A **Raw Frequency Analysis Chart** displays this information in chart form. You extract data from the frequency analysis to identify numbers that you will use in your tickets under the theory that there is a bias in how prior numbers were drawn or that there is a tendency of certain numbers to appear more often than others, either in the long run or short term.

Frequency analysis allows you to identify the trends, streaks, tendencies, best numbers, overdue balls, clusters, combinations and a host of other data that you will extract and use to form your winning strategies. In addition to these core strategies, you rely on frequency analysis to identify the various keys—such as kings, queens and exotic numbers—that you will use in the Level II strategies.

In running a frequency analysis, you can choose as many games from a regression history as are available. Computer strategies have many advantages over traditional hand-created databases, but the most compelling one is the ability to populate, store and analyze huge databases of previous winning balls.

All strategies for lotto games in both the powerful Level 1 core strategies and the advanced Level II key strategies rely on the results of frequency analysis.

HOW TO MAKE FREQUENCY ANALYSIS CHARTS

To create a Raw Frequency Analysis Chart, you start with a blank chart created specifically for this purpose. In the left column, you list the balls in the pool of numbers. In the second column, you record the balls as they appear, using dots or vertical lines to indicate a drawn ball (or whatever notation you're comfortable with). It's pretty much the same chart we used for the lottery, except here, we only show one position.

FREQUENCY ANALYSIS
Blank Worksheet

1	
2	
3	
4	
5	
6	
7	
8	
9	
10	
11	
12	
13	
14	
15	
16	
17	
18	
19	
20	
21	
22	
23	
24	
25	

For example, if the 16 is drawn, you indicate this next to the 16 by making a dot. You will keep filling in the numbers drawn until all the columns have been completed. The last column will be saved for totaling the occurrences, adding all the results in a left to right manner.

You do not break down balls by position, as in the Positional Charts for lottery games, because there is only one pool and all balls come from that same pool. You only care about total frequency, which is why these charts are called Frequency Analysis Charts.

In this particular analysis, you are going to record the numbers in groups of 25 drawings. There are four columns for each of these groups and a final column to record the results of each number over that 100-game span (four groups of twenty-five games each). You use four tally rows so that you can keep both shorter-term and longer-term histories at the same time. This is a good habit to get into because when you take forays into advanced Level III strategies, the greater amount of data gives you more flexibility to make advanced plays.

But first, let's chart some more winning draws.

In addition to the 16, let's say that the next five balls drawn in a six-ball game are 21, 24, 3, 8 and 17. You would record the numbers on your worksheet.

The following page shows the first drawing recorded. The subsequent page shows 25 draws recorded. You see how the worksheet starts to fill up with data.

RAW FREQUENCY ANALYSIS CHART
Dot Results / 1 Lotto Game

1	
2	
3	•
4	
5	
6	
7	
8	•
9	
10	
11	
12	
13	
14	
15	
16	•
17	•
18	
19	
20	
21	•
22	
23	
24	•
25	

RAW FREQUENCY ANALYSIS CHART
25 Games / 6/25 Lotto Game

1	•••••••••••
2	•••••
3	••••
4	•
5	•••••••••
6	•••••••
7	•••
8	••••••
9	•••••••
10	•••••••
11	•••
12	••••••••
13	••• ••
14	••••••••
15	••••••••••
16	••
17	•••••
18	•••••••
19	••••••
20	•••••
21	••••••••
22	••••••••
23	•••
24	••••••••••
25	••••••••

There will be 150 marks per column (25 games multiplied by six numbers per game), and 600 marks in all since you are charting four columns. Twenty-five games is not a lot of data to work with, but as more games get added to the database, dots begin to fill more densely into your charts and you begin to see more established patterns form than those that you observed after just 10 games.

The structure of the chart allows you to observe both short term (25 games) and longer term (100 games) trends and patterns. With 100 games on your chart, you could work with the four groups of 25 games, break this data up into 10-game increments, or use the entire block of 100 games as your regression analysis. When you break down a larger sample of data to analyze it in smaller blocks of 25 drawings, it is called a **quadrant analysis**; and when you break that data down into smaller blocks of 10 drawings (**decades**), it is called a **decades analysis**. There are advanced strategies in the back of this book that are specifically designed to exploit decade and quadrant trends, but for now, I'll give you a brief look at a quadrant analysis chart.

You'll see that the results in this quadrant analysis give you a good insight into how the numbers are flowing. The chart on the prior page used dots to indicate every time a number had been drawn over a 25-game regression. The chart on the following page converts those dots to numbers so that the results are easy to see and use. You'll see that conversion in the first quadrant along with the results in number form from three more quadrants so that a full 100 games can be analyzed. These 100 drawings are actual results compiled at the end of December 2015 from West Virginia's Cash25, a 6/25 lotto game (six balls drawn from a pool of 25 balls).

REFINED FREQUENCY ANALYSIS CHART
100 Games / 6/25 Lotto Game

Number	1-25	26-50	51-75	76-100	Totals
1	11	7	7	7	32
2	5	5	5	4	19
3	4	3	8	7	22
4	1	8	9	7	25
5	9	3	8	7	27
6	6	9	4	10	29
7	3	1	4	7	15
8	5	6	3	4	18
9	7	10	5	8	30
10	6	8	4	10	28
11	3	5	6	6	20
12	8	6	8	8	30
13	5	4	5	4	18
14	7	11	5	6	29
15	9	3	8	3	23
16	2	6	4	7	19
17	5	5	4	5	19
18	6	10	4	4	24
19	6	6	8	5	25
20	5	3	9	6	23
21	8	4	6	5	23
22	8	6	2	4	20
23	3	4	5	3	15
24	9	6	9	6	30
25	8	11	9	6	34

BEST NUMBER FREQUENCY ANALYSIS

The Raw Frequency Analysis (similar to the Positional Analysis for lottery) charts raw data that needs to be converted and refined into more usable charts, such as Best Number and Overdue Analyses.

A **Best Number Frequency Analysis** sorts the data from a Raw Frequency Analysis Chart by order of frequency with the hottest number listed first, the second-hottest number listed second, and so on. It is helpful to use a quadrant chart for the 100-game analysis so that you can examine recent trends and early trends. **Recent trends** indicate patterns that have occurred in the last quarter or so of drawings—or quadrant, in a quadrant analysis—while **early trends** indicate patterns that have occurred in the first half of an analysis; for example, the first five decades (50 games) of drawings in a decade analysis of 100 games.

On certain advanced analyses and Level III strategies, you might also run decades charts to get a micro look at the trends. In a decades analysis, you divide the 100-game block of drawings into 11 columns, 10 of the columns for the decades, and the last, eleventh one, for the totals.

Here is a Best Number Frequency Analysis divided into four groups—quadrants. The numbers are listed in order from most frequently drawn (at the top) to least frequently drawn (at the bottom).

BEST NUMBER FREQUENCY ANALYSIS
By Quadrants / 100 6/25 Lotto Games

1-25		26-50		51-75		76-100		Quadrants
#	Frq	#	Frq	#	Frq	#	Frq	Best Number
1	11	14	11	4	9	6	10	Most Draws
5	9	25	11	20	9	10	10	2nd
15	9	9	10	24	9	9	8	3rd
24	9	18	10	25	9	12	8	4th
12	8	6	9	3	8	1	7	5th
21	8	4	8	5	8	3	7	6th
22	8	10	8	12	8	4	7	7th
25	8	1	7	15	8	5	7	8th
9	7	T*	6	19	8	7	7	9th
14	7	-	-	1	7	16	7	10th

*Six numbers tied at six draws each—8, 10, 16, 19, 22 and 24

It is interesting to see the distribution of numbers as provided by a quadrant analysis. It opens up the possibilities for analysis and advanced strategies. This Best Number Frequency Analysis from West Virginia's Cash25, a 6/25 lotto game I tracked in December 2015 charts about six months of prior results. It lists the hottest numbers, by quadrant, in order of most frequently drawn to least frequently drawn.

Only the top 10 best numbers are shown. You don't need to display all of them since you will only be playing the top two numbers anyway.

BEST NUMBER FREQUENCY ANALYSIS
100 Games / 6/25 Lotto Game

Best Number	Frequency	Rank
25	34	1
1	32	2
9	30	3
12	30	4
24	30	5
6	29	6
14	29	7
10	28	8
5	27	9
4	25	10
19	25	11
18	24	12
15	23	13
20	23	14
21	23	15
3	22	16
11	20	17
22	20	18
2	19	19
16	19	20
17	19	21
8	18	22
13	18	23
7	15	24
23	15	25

OVERDUE FREQUENCY ANALYSIS

An **Overdue Frequency Analysis** sorts the data from a Raw Frequency Analysis Chart by order of least frequency over a specified period of time—the opposite of a Best Number Frequency Analysis. The number with the fewest total of occurrences is listed first, the second fewest total of occurrences second, and so on down to the 10 numbers ranked by fewest number of occurrences.

The chart also shows the number of times that the overdue numbers have been drawn. While you only care about the 10 most overdue numbers, or perhaps the 12 or so most overdue, sometimes you want to expand your analysis to the top 20 or so, because overdue numbers are very fluid. As you go from one drawing to the following drawing, your overdue numbers might start getting hit (which is why you are playing them!) and other numbers outside your top chosen numbers, for example, may rise to the top. In the Overdue Frequency Analysis Chart that follows, I'm showing the top 10 most overdue candidates

As before, we run a quadrant analysis so that you can spot recent trends and early trends in your 100-game regression. This gives you the flexibility to play both Level I and Level II strategies, as well as exotic Level III strategies as well. We'll also run a full overdue analysis for the full 100 game regression. That chart will follow the quadrant analysis.

OVERDUE FREQUENCY ANALYSIS CHART
Quadrant Analysis / 100 6/25 Lotto Games

1-25		26-50		51-75		76-100		Quadrants
#	Frq	#	Frq	#	Frq	#	Frq	Overdue
4	1	7	1	22	2	15	3	Fewest Draws
16	2	3	3	8	3	2	4	2nd
7	3	5	3	6	4	8	4	3rd
11	3	15	3	7	4	13	4	4th
23	3	20	3	10	4	18	4	5th
3	4	13	4	16	4	22	4	6th
2	5	21	4	17	4	17	5	7th
8	5	23	4	18	4	19	5	8th
13	5	T**	5	***	5	21	5	9th
17	5*	-	-	-	-	++	6	10th

*The 20 in the 1st column also was drawn five times.
**Three numbers in the 2nd column tied at five draws—2, 11, and 17.
***Five numbers in the 3rd column tied at five draws—5, 9, 13, 14, and 23.
++Five numbers in the 4th column tied at six draws—11, 14, 20, 24, and 25.

This Overdue Frequency Analysis from West Virginia's Cash25, a 6/25 lotto game, charts about six months of prior results as of December 2015. This chart compiles those results and lists the most overdue numbers, by quadrant, in order of least frequently drawn to most frequently drawn.

Only the top 10 most overdue numbers are shown.

OVERDUE FREQUENCY ANALYSIS
100 Games / 6/25 Lotto Game

Best Number	Frequency	Rank
23	15	1
7	15	2
13	18	3
8	18	4
17	19	5
16	19	6
2	19	7
22	20	8
11	20	9
3	22	10
21	23	11
20	23	12
15	23	13
18	24	14
19	25	15
4	25	16
5	27	17
10	28	18
14	29	19
6	29	20
24	30	21
12	30	22
9	30	23
1	32	24
25	34	25

Your overdue charts will change rapidly as cold numbers get drawn and are no longer overdue, so you must keep on top of your numbers, game by game. For example, if the previously cold number 46 was drawn, you might have to move it down your most overdue list. If it was drawn a second time in succession, you would certainly be moving it down your overdue numbers list, and likely would move it right onto your best number list!

As you have seen, Overdue Number Charts track the frequency of numbers being drawn over a specified number of games. But there is another way to chart overdue numbers — by length of time since the number has been drawn. I have developed specialized strategies to mine these opportunities. These are powerful tools for overdue players. There are even more powerful tools you can use to form Level III strategies called *Complex Distance Charts*. (You can find out more information about them in the back pages of this book.)

Now let's turn our attention to the next Level I core strategy: Cluster Analysis.

CLUSTER ANALYSIS

Cluster analysis is the science of charting and statistically identifying and analyzing balls that have been drawn together in a specified number of individual lotto or lottery drawings and displays them in order from most frequently drawn to least frequently drawn. Numbers drawn together in an individual lotto or lottery drawing are called **clusters** or **paired numbers**.

ORGANIZING CLUSTERS

You want to identify all the clusters (paired groups) from this drawing. Let's say you're following a six-ball lotto game and the following numbers have been drawn:

In Order of Draw	Sorted
9 17 3 43 11 47	3 9 11 17 43 47

Let's identify the paired groups that have been drawn together in this lotto. You'll display the paired groups in ascending order showing every possible combination. You do this not only because winning numbers are displayed this way, but also because it is easier to identify the clusters. Remember, it doesn't matter in which order the balls are drawn, only that they were drawn.

You always display paired groups by the smaller number first. Here are the paired groups:

CLUSTER COMBINATION CHART

Paired Groups (Clusters)				Groupings
3 9	3 11	3 17	3 43	3 47	("3" grouping)
9 11	9 17	9 43	9 47		("9" grouping)
11 17		11 43	11 47		("11" grouping)
17 43		17 47			("17" grouping)
43 47					("43" grouping)

Grouping classifies the paired numbers in a drawing by referencing the **anchor ball**, the lowest numbered ball in a cluster. You identify a cluster group first by naming its anchor ball. The first grouping, the "3" grouping, indicates that the 3 is the anchor ball. The highest numbered ball in a cluster is called the **chain ball**.

As you can see, the anchor ball of 3—that is, in the 3 grouping—has chain balls of 9, 11, 17, 43 and 47.

Technically, it doesn't matter whether a cluster is displayed as 3 9 or 9 3, or 43 47 or 47 43. In any of these cases, the two balls are drawn together so they are clusters. However, to keep your clusters organized and easy to match, you display them in ascending order. In the parenthesis after each cluster line, I have added the term "the 'X' grouping." I have added the term "'X' grouping," with the X standing for the anchor ball in each cluster. For example, the first line in the Cluster Combination Chart lists the "3" grouping. This indicates that the anchor ball in the cluster group is a 3.

To organize clusters, start with the lowest number and add combinations of every other drawn number. Then take the second lowest number and do the same, omitting any duplicates. Then the third number, fourth number and fifth number. You can't do this with the sixth number because it will be identical to the first, which you have already recorded. The lowest number will have five unique combinations; the second lowest will have four combinations; the third lowest, three combinations; the fourth lowest, two combinations; and the fifth lowest, one combination—just like you see in the Cluster Combination Chart.

There are 15 total unique clusters in this six-ball drawing. In all six-ball drawings, there will be exactly 15 unique clusters. In a five-ball drawing, there will be exactly 10 unique clusters.

Here is a breakdown on cluster groups in a six-ball lotto game, and then a five-ball lotto game:

CLUSTER GROUPINGS
SIX-BALL LOTTO

Number	Groupings
Lowest	5
2nd Lowest	4
3rd Lowest	3
4th Lowest	2
5th Lowest	1
Total	15

CLUSTER GROUPINGS
FIVE-BALL LOTTO

Number	Groupings
Lowest	4
2nd Lowest	3
3rd Lowest	2
4th Lowest	1
Total	10

Game	Cluster Groupings
5-Ball Game	10
6-Ball Game	15

FIVE-BALL DRAW EXAMPLE

In Order of Draw	Sorted
27 1 15 13 30	1 13 15 27 30

CLUSTER COMBINATION CHART

Paired Groups (Clusters)			Groupings
1 13| 1 15	1 27	1 30	("1" Grouping)
13 15	13 27	13 30	("13" Grouping)
15 27	15 30		("15" Grouping)
27 30			("36" Grouping)

REPEATING CLUSTERS

What you're looking for in a cluster analysis are **repeating clusters**; that is, two numbers that get drawn together in two or more drawings over a specified number of games. For example, the cluster pairs 11 and 14 might appear in two different drawings. That is a repeating cluster. These are the most powerful cluster formations. There are other types of cluster formations, but the repeating clusters are the ones on which you will concentrate.

Let's look at three drawing groups and identify the clusters. The numbers have been sorted in ascending order.

A DRAWING	B DRAWING	C DRAWING
14 17 19 26 45 47	2 14 19 26 28 40	2 8 12 26 31 40

REPEATING CLUSTERS

A & B DRAWING	B & C DRAWING
Repeating Clusters	**Repeating Clusters**
14 17 **19** 26 45 47	**2** 14 19 26 28 **40**
2 **14 19** 26 28 40	**2** 8 12 26 31 **40**

In the A and B drawings, 14 and 19 were repeating clusters, and in the B and C drawing, 2 and 40 were repeating clusters. In the diagram, the repeating clusters are shown in bold type.

These are just three sample drawings, hardly much of a sample, but they serve the purpose of showing you how to recognize repeating clusters. As you add more drawings, the process of identifying repeating clusters gets unwieldy, if not brain scrambling, since there are 15 clusters in each draw. This is why you really prefer computer software specifically set up to identify clusters as opposed to identifying clusters by hand.

You can still identify repeating clusters by hand—but it's just a lot of work!

To be useful, a cluster analysis requires a much larger sample of games than just three games because repeating clusters don't come up that frequently. It would not be unusual for a handful of draws to have no repeating clusters.

INCORRECT CLUSTER METHOD VS. CORRECT CLUSTER METHOD

One school of thought, let's call it the **Incorrect Clusters Method**, holds that the numbers must be drawn sequentially; that is, one ball following the other. You can only identify these types of clusters if the order of balls picked is displayed in the results. However, if they are displayed in ascending order from lowest numbered ball to highest, as they are normally done, you would be unable to identify the cluster because you have no way of knowing the order in which the balls were drawn.

But it doesn't matter—you don't care about the order of balls drawn in five-ball or six-ball lotto games. All the balls come from the same pool!

The proper way to choose clustered numbers is to examine the pool of numbers from the same drawing as a group, regardless of order. We'll call this the **Correct Clusters Method**. For your purposes, it is statistically irrelevant in which order balls were drawn, you only care that particular balls were drawn.

Let's compare the Incorrect Cluster Method and the correct one so that you can see the flaws in the incorrect model. We'll go back to our "A," "B," and "C" drawings. We showed the drawings sorted in ascending order.

SORTED IN ASCENDING ORDER		
A DRAWING	**B DRAWING**	**C DRAWING**
14 17 19 26 45 47	2 14 19 26 28 40	2 8 12 26 31 40

As pointed out, in the A and B drawings, 14 and 19 were repeating clusters, and in the B and C drawing, 2 and 40 were as well. But the actual order of drawing was as follows:

EXACTLY AS DRAWN		
A DRAWING	**B DRAWING**	**C DRAWING**
45 26 14 17 47 19	2 26 28 40 14 19	8 40 12 31 26 2

The Correct Method found repeating clusters in the A and B drawings and in the B and C drawings, while the incorrect method fails to identify a single cluster. If you were playing clusters, you would have missed *two* valuable paired numbers!

WEIGHTING NUMBERS
FREQUENCY OF NUMBERS AND WEIGHTING

In the Level I strategies, you are going to play your numbers across the tickets in a fairly even distribution. In other words, each number you have chosen to play—that is, your chosen numbers—will be played about as often as the other numbers in your final pool.

Let's say you have chosen these nine numbers to play:

$$5, 21, 22, 27, 32, 34, 41, 42, 44$$

So, if number 5 is played on eight tickets, the other numbers will also be played on about eight tickets as well. Some will only distribute to seven tickets because the math may not divide evenly. In other words, in a normal distribution, your chosen numbers would appear on either seven or eight tickets.

How do you decide which ones go on eight tickets and which ones on seven tickets? This is a case where you don't want to outthink yourself or go crazy deciding what is what and which is which. Play them as they fall, some on eight tickets, some on seven tickets.

If you have more confidence in some numbers than others, make those numbers the ones that hit the eight tickets.

My basic point: Play your numbers and tickets as they come out. Don't drive yourself batty on minutia.

UNBALANCED RANDOM WEIGHTING

Using our example above, of the nine chosen numbers, you may decide, for no particular reason, to play some numbers on seven or nine tickets with the majority being played on eight tickets and perhaps a few on just six tickets. This is called **unbalanced random weighting**. You can play tickets in this fashion, but the ideal manner is to get your chosen numbers as equally distributed as you can.

When uneven weighting is by design, it is an entirely different story! Now, because you are scientifically and strategically using real criteria to create uneven weights, you play some numbers on more tickets than others. Unbalanced weighting by design is a powerful and advanced strategy we will cover in the following chapter.

Stay tuned!

LOTTERY AND LOTTO ANALYSIS REVIEW

I have covered a lot in this chapter, but I only want to review the two most important strategies so that you don't get confused. Because of the way the games are structured, the basic core strategies you rely on to identify your chosen numbers in lottery and lotto games are different. In the lottery, you identify numbers by tracking the position in which they are drawn (as opposed to 1,000 numbers as a whole in three-ball games, or 10,000 numbers in the four-ball game), while in the lotto you look at the actual full number chosen.

Each of these games requires a different analysis to correctly isolate the patterns you would use in your strategies. For the three-ball and four-ball lottery game strategies, you rely on a positional analysis. For the five-ball and six-ball game strategies, you rely on a frequency analysis as the baseline analysis. I have covered these in detail in this chapter.

The multi-state games, such as Powerball and Mega Millions, are combo games—hybrids—which rely on a combination of the positional and frequency analyses. I will cover those strategies in Chapter 13, *Dual-Pool Level III Lottery Strategies.*

CORE STRATEGY BY GAME

Game	Type	Core Strategy
Scratch-Off	Instant	Pure Luck
3 Ball	Lottery	Positional Analysis
4 Ball	Lottery	Positional Analysis
5 Ball	Lotto	Frequency Analysis
6 Ball	Lotto	Frequency Analysis
5+1	Multi-state*	Frequency & Positional

*Includes games such as Powerball, Mega Millions, Hot Lotto, Lucky for Life, Wild Card 2, 2by2, MegaHits, Tri-State Megabucks Plus

NEXT STEPS

In this chapter, we've identified best (hot) numbers, overdue (cold) numbers, and clusters—the core strategies you will use to identify the best-performing numbers. Now, what do you do with these numbers? That's the question, but I have answers for you.

Read on! It's time to delve deeper into the meat of choosing your optimal lottery and lotto tickets. You are about to enter the advanced world of using keys to make tickets.

8

LEVEL II STRATEGIES: KEY NUMBERS

Before you move on to the Level II strategies in this chapter, the keys, you must have a firm grasp of the Level I core strategies we just covered. They are the foundation you build everything else on. You rely on the Level I strategies to tell you the most important numbers to play—your chosen numbers. The Level II strategies that we'll cover here identify the most important of your chosen numbers—or bring in numbers from outside that group—and treat these numbers in a more aggressive or *more important* fashion, if you will.

The basic tenet of the Level I strategies is that you are going to play your chosen numbers more or less equally across the board. With Level II strategies, you are using advanced analyses to identify a special number or numbers in which you have the highest confidence level. You give these special numbers an unequal and greater weighting than the other numbers you are going to play so that they will appear on more tickets than the regular pool of chosen numbers.

The Level II plays are advanced enhancements of the Level I strategies. Think of it this way: The Level I strategies are the body, engine and basic components of a car you are building.

The Level II strategies provide the engine with enhancements that give your car another gear and more power. You need your car for basic driving, but you also want the power to take it to another level.

You will still rely on Best Number Analysis, Overdue Number Analysis, cluster analysis, frequency analysis, positional analysis and your other tools, but now you're going to work extra magic within those parameters and, sometimes, *outside* those parameters to form even stronger tickets.

In this chapter, you're going to learn how to identify and use king numbers, queen numbers, and wizards, plus how to implement lucky numbers and combine all these powerful plays with Level I strategies. You'll now have the basis for stepping into the rarified air of the exclusive Level III strategies, which we'll cover after this chapter. Just as Level II strategies rely on Level I strategies to make optimal tickets, the Level III strategies rely on Level II plays.

In a nutshell, Level II strategies give you the tools to identify, extract and use important numbers so that they can be incorporated into your Level I core strategies. This allows you to have an even more aggressive set of numbers to go after big jackpots, as well as the ability to try to accumulate a conglomeration of small wins to fuel the system as you patiently, or impatiently, wait for the real goal of trying to land a huge multimillion-dollar jackpot. Those big jackpots don't come around often and few players ever get the thrill of winning one, but the Level II strategies will keep you in the hunt.

First, let's understand the concept of a *key number*, the central foundation of the Level II strategies.

KEY NUMBERS

A **key number** is the most important number or numbers among tickets you will play in a lottery or lotto game, one that will get played more frequently than your other chosen numbers. The key has the highest confidence level of any number and creates an unbalanced weighting—that is, the key will be on more tickets than other chosen numbers—because it is a more valuable number than its counterparts. In a wheel (which I will cover later) or group of tickets, the key will be the centerpiece of the numbers you will use to create winners. Think of it as the sun (the key) around which the other planets (chosen numbers) revolve.

A key number will be played on most if not all the tickets you play and in a greater frequency than your regular chosen numbers. You have the most confidence in your key numbers based on the strategies you're playing and therefore, all your other chosen numbers, while still important enough to be played, play second fiddle to the key number. There are various categories of key numbers, depending upon how you'll be using them in your tickets. When a key number is played on every ticket, it is called a **master key** number. Master key numbers, by dint of being on all tickets, will be the most important number of all the numbers you play.

You can sometimes have multiple key numbers, either of equal strength to each other or in decreasing strength. Multiple key numbers of equal strength will be played in equal frequency on your tickets. For example, if you're playing 10 tickets, nine or 10 of those tickets will contain the key numbers.

With multiple key numbers of decreasing strength—say 15, 18 and 41 are your keys, for example—you might play the 15 on all 10 tickets, the 18 on nine of them, and the 41 on eight of the tickets, in addition to your other chosen numbers. In this instance, the 15 is the most important key number in a multiple-key ticket group, so it is the **major key number**; the second most important number is 18, which is the **minor key**; and the 41, which is a more important number than your regular chosen numbers, is known as the **third key number** because it plays third fiddle to the major and minor key numbers.

There are other types of key numbers but I will only cover these four categories—master, major, minor, and third keys—in this chapter.

Your key number can be a number that you have identified from a Level I core analysis that you have run, or a number that you have extracted from another type of analysis.

But in all cases, key numbers are the strongest numbers in your tickets.

KEY NUMBER CATEGORIES

Master Key: A key number played on every ticket.
Major Key: The most important key number in a multiple-key ticket group.
Minor Key: The second most important number in a multiple-key ticket group.
Third Key: The third most important number in a multiple-key ticket group.

ONE KEY OR MULTIPLE KEYS?

You will encounter many situations where you have identified a number or multiple numbers that could be designated as key numbers, meaning that you will give them more weight than the regular chosen numbers.

Your quandary: Do you play just one key or do you incorporate a second or third key into your tickets?

You have to set your own baseline for the concept of *importance*. You are going to give a key a high priority because it has greatly exceeded the standards for which you have selected for your chosen numbers—or because, for some other reason, you have determined a particular number has a priority over the other numbers you will be playing. In some of the keys discussed below, I will outline specific criteria for playing keys. You can choose to play keys, or not, depending on the parameters you set for your strategies.

I am outlining many strategies and tactics in this book and showing you how to use them. You have to determine the philosophy with which you will attack the lottery and lotto games, whether or not you want to use keys, and the overall strategies you will use to form tickets.

Bottom line: If you have an exceedingly important number, you want it as a key. If you have identified an additional number or two in which you have *great* confidence, as opposed to *strong* confidence (your regular chosen numbers), you have the option to elevate these chosen numbers to keys. In that instance, you might work with minor and third keys for your tickets. In the *Wheeling Strategy* chapter, I will talk more about how to use keys in your tickets.

So how do you decide whether to use a master key that gets used on all the tickets, or simply a major key, your high-confidence number that gets used on most, but not all, tickets?

Let's look at that now.

MASTER KEYS VS. MAJOR KEYS

Okay, you've chosen your numbers and are preparing to arrange them into a formidable group of tickets. The Level I strategies call for giving about an equal coverage to your chosen numbers, and the Level II strategies call for weighting certain numbers; that is, playing some numbers on more tickets than others.

So how much weight do you give a number? What is your confidence level? Do you make your most important number a key and if so, do you make it a master key or a major key?

How you handle these things comes down to your philosophy of betting tickets or, when playing an advanced Level III strategy, the dictates of the strategy itself. If you think that a particular number (or numbers) is so strong that it must be played on every ticket, you make it a master key. If you feel this number is strong but doesn't deserve that kind of priority—that is, you don't have supreme confidence in its strength and you want to have other tickets in the mix to cover occasions when your master doesn't appear—then you want to downgrade your master key to a major key to maintain flexibility in ticket coverage.

Again, if you're playing certain Level III strategies, they will spell out the requirements needed to promote chosen numbers to keys, and how you would play those keys on your tickets.

MASTER KEY VS. MAJOR KEY
Strengths and Weaknesses

Master Key Strength

The strength of designating a master key is that you are taking your very best number, a number that has your highest confidence, and building tickets around its strength. It's a confident approach and a strong one—building around your best.

Master Key Weakness

For you to win the big jackpot, your master key must be part of the winning ticket. If your master is not one of the balls drawn, you can't win the jackpot, plus your chances of winning the lesser prizes are weakened and are more dependent on your other keys or chosen numbers.

Major Key Strength

The beauty of a major key is that you take your best number and build around that number while still maintaining the flexibility of a backup plan. If your major key doesn't hit, you still have other tickets out there that can bring home the big bacon; and if your major key hits, you're well covered to have a shot.

Major Key Weakness

By not having a master on your best number, you leave open a few holes in your backup chosen numbers, holes that would be covered if your master key gets drawn. But that's a sacrifice you make for the flexibility of playing a major key instead of a master key.

LEVEL II
KEY-NUMBER STRATEGIES

Using key numbers is a central part of advanced winning strategies. A key number can be derived from any type of analysis. Your goal in the Level II strategies is to identify the number or numbers that you will give the greatest confidence to.

Not all numbers are equal. If they were, you wouldn't bother to isolate the chosen numbers that fall into the various trends that you uncover in your analyses, nor the special ones among that pool. It is important to understand that not only are some numbers better than others, *some numbers are much better than others*. In a war, the opposing general is the most important enemy to capture because he is the most powerful player in the grid. He has the greatest influence. That general, in terms of a lottery number analogy, is your major key—the most important piece in the battle.

Let's say you're running a Best Number Analysis. You extract the results and discover that one number was drawn at a much higher frequency than the other numbers. Let's say that number is 22. In your analysis, the 22 is your best candidate. In the Level 1 strategies, you treat the 22 equally to the other best numbers you're going to work with. You do not distinguish that number from any other chosen number.

However, in the Level II strategies you seek to isolate numbers that are *special*; that is, they have greatly outperformed their peers. And since these numbers are special, you treat them that way and play them with greater emphasis in your tickets. In this example, the number 22 is the number you would build around.

I discussed the various types of keys you could promote from your pool of chosen numbers—master, major, minor and third keys—now you will see how to identify those special numbers that have outperformed their peers and which you will promote to keys.

BEST NUMBERS & KEYS

A Best Number Analysis identifies the hottest numbers over a specified number of games. You might choose a regression level of 25 games, for example, or even 50 games or 100 games. Over any regression level, certain numbers will stand out as the best performers and these are the numbers you will identify and take note of for your strategies.

The very best performing number of a Best Number Analysis, the most frequently drawn number, is called the **king**, the **queen** is the second-best performing number, and the third-best performer is called a **court**.

When the first or second-best performers are tied for frequency, the most recently drawn number is designated as the king and the second-most recently drawn number is designated as the queen. The same applies to the other numbers. For example, if two numbers are tied for second-most draws, say the 9 and 39, the 39 will be the queen after you observe that it was the last number drawn, and the 9 will be the court.

Let's reprise the 100-game Best Number Analysis for the West Virginia 6/25 game from earlier and see if we can find some keys. We'll just show the top ten results.

BEST NUMBER FREQUENCY ANALYSIS
100 Games / 6/25 Lotto Game

Best Number	Frequency	Rank
25	34	1
1	32	2
9	30	3
12	30	4
24	30	5
6	29	6
14	29	7
10	28	8
5	27	9
4	25	10

PROMOTING KINGS

The best performing number is the 25. That is the king. A very good number—your best number—but is it good enough to elevate to a major or master key number? To promote a king to a key, the king must satisfy the following two criteria for a 100 game regression level. You use the 3-6 rule.

1. The king must have been drawn at least three more times than the third best performing number.
2. The king must have been drawn at least six more games than the tenth best performing number.

If the king fits both of these criteria, it has proven itself to excel in the results over its nearest rivals and attains the status of a key, an important number you will play on most if not all of your tickets. If the king does not fit both of the criteria above, it is not strong enough to be promoted to a key. In that instance, it should be treated as just another chosen number (and not be given special treatment) in the formation of your tickets.

PROMOTING QUEENS

When there is a king that has been promoted to a key—and only when that king has been promoted—the next-best performing number, the queen, is automatically promoted to a key as well, regardless of the number of draws. You cannot promote a queen to a key when the better performing number, the king, has not been promoted. You always want to use your best numbers to play your tickets, so when there is a king key, there is a queen key, but when there is no king key, there is no queen key. The queen always promotes with the king.

> **When there is a king key, there is a queen key, but when there is no king key, there is no queen key.**

KING & QUEEN PROMOTION EXAMPLE

The top results of a Best Number Analysis show that the 25 is your king and the 1 is your queen. They are the two best-performing numbers. Let's see if the king fits the criteria to elevate to a key. You always start with the king to see if it can promote to a key because without a king key, there is no queen key.

The first criterion is that, "The king must have been drawn at least three more times than the third best performing number." This condition is met, since 34 draws is four more draws than 30 draws.

The second criterion states that, "The king must have been drawn at least six more times than the tenth best performing number." There is a nine-number difference, so this criterion is easily met as well.

You promote the king to a key!

The king is now a key number you'll build around. The queen, the 8 ball, is automatically promoted to a queen for your second key.

Number	Draws		Promotion
25	34	(King)	Key
1	30	(Queen)	Key

KINGS AND QUEENS

Now that you have had a king promotion along with the automatic queen promotion, you have two keys in play and must decide how to use them. You think about it for a while and mull your options. You can choose to play a single key using the king number, though I recommend sending the full royalty into action using the king as a major (or master) key and the queen as a minor key. These two powerful keys can be used to fully attack your set of tickets.

Note that kings and queens that have been promoted to keys should always be played more intensely than your regular chosen numbers in Level II strategies. They are your very top performing numbers.

COURTS

Notice that we did not discuss court numbers in our conversations about kings, queens and keys. The reason is that that the courts can be used in multiple ways, depending upon your philosophy and what you're trying to do with them. As the third-most important number in your frequency and positional analyses, they have serious oomph. They are proven winners—after all, they are the most frequently drawn numbers after the king and queen—and pack a lot of possibilities toward a package of potential winning tickets.

Some lottery players view the courts as rising stars. There are even specialized Level III court strategies that focus on what some players consider the most exciting number in the spectrum of numbers available—that is, one of the very best hot numbers, but not overplayed.

Aggressive players also frequently use courts as keys to fill their tickets, and sometimes even use **fourths** as keys, the fourth-best performing number in a Best Number Analysis.

Let's take a quick look at some ways that courts can be played.

1. When you're looking to play a third key, you'll use a court because, of course, it is your third-most important number.

2. If you're looking to play a very aggressive group of tickets, you can promote the court to a minor key.

3. In some Level III strategies, the court can take on a more aggressive, interesting and vital role in the formation of tickets. Of course, you'll play courts as keys in those instances.

BEST (HOT) NUMBER DESIGNATIONS

King	Hottest number
Queen	Second hottest number
Court	The third hottest number

What happens when two or more numbers are tied for the third position—which one do you promote to the court? In fact, that is exactly what has occurred in the 100-game regression for the West Virginia Cash25 lotto game. The 9, 12, and 24 all were drawn 30 times each over that span. Even though these three balls have been drawn an equal number of times the 9 is your court since it not only was the most recently drawn, but had been drawn three times in the last five drawings. In case of ties, you always use the most recently drawn number as the tiebreaker in a Best Number Analysis.

OVERDUE NUMBERS & KEYS

DUKES, EARLS & COLD COURTS

The *duke* and *earl* keys are foils to the king and queen keys. They represent the most overdue numbers, the opposite of the best numbers represented by the king and queen. In an Overdue Number Analysis, the **duke** represents the most overdue (coldest) number, that is, the least frequently drawn number (coldest) in a specified number of games. and the **earl** represents the second-least frequently drawn number.

When you use dukes and earls, you always play them as important keys on the cold spectrum of plays, much as you would play kings and queens on the hot spectrum.

To promote a duke to a key, the most overdue number must outperform the third most overdue number, the **cold court**, by a separation of three games. So if the duke has not been drawn in 20 games and the cold court, the third most overdue number, has not been drawn in 17 games, the duke will be promoted to a key, which automatically promotes the next-best performing number, the earl, into a key as well.

Just as you must have the king to have a queen, the duke must be a key for the earl to be a key as well. In other words, you can't have an earl key unless you have a duke key.

In the Overdue Frequency Analysis from West Virginia's Cash25 game, we see that the 23, along with the 7 are the most overdue numbers. They have been drawn only 15 times over the 100-game regressions level. But are they candidates for a key?

Let's take a look.

You compare the two numbers and see that there is just enough separation between the duke and the cold court for this level of regression. The duke, your top performing overdue number, has been drawn exactly three fewer times than the third most overdue number, the 13 (and 8), and qualifies to be promoted to to a key.

OVERDUE FREQUENCY ANALYSIS
100 Games / 6/25 Lotto Game

Best Number	Frequency	Rank
23	15	1
7	15	2
13	18	3
8	18	4
17	19	5
16	19	6
2	19	7
22	20	8
11	20	9
3	22	10

OVERDUE NUMBER DESIGNATIONS

Duke	The most overdue number
Earl	The second-most overdue number
Cold Court	The third-most overdue number

LUCKY ANALYSIS & LUCKY NUMBERS

Let's say that you like a particular number or a few numbers that you arrived at by whatever means. Some numbers are just *lucky* in your life, or at least you feel that they are lucky right now. Many players want to play **lucky numbers**—any numbers that a player feels is lucky for him or her and wants to incorporate them into their tickets. **Lucky Analysis** gives you the freedom of inputting your own "lucky" numbers into the tickets you'll play.

You do this by promoting your lucky numbers to keys.

If you're going to play these numbers, you can run them through our lucky analysis filters and play them alongside Level I core strategy chosen numbers on your tickets.

While you can group lucky numbers in among your chosen numbers, many players treat them as special. If you are one of these players, you will want to slot the lucky numbers into your pool as preferential plays—that is, as keys. When you choose two lucky numbers to enter into your wheel or playing tickets, you designate them as the **big luck** number and the **little luck** number, respectively. Usually, the big luck will be given greater strength in your tickets, and the little luck a lesser preference, though they could both be played with equal strength. A third lucky number is called a **side luck** number.

LUCKY NUMBER DESIGNATIONS

Big Luck	Your most important lucky number
Little Luck	Your second most important lucky number
Side Luck	Your third most important number

I recommend that if you're using one lucky number, you treat the big luck number as a major key, though you could elevate it into a master key covering all the numbers; and if there is a second lucky number you must play, the little luck, you treat that number as a minor key. If there is yet one more number to play, the side luck, then you'll slot the side luck in as a third key.

WIZARDS

The *wizard* is an elusive Level II key that requires extra effort to discover. It takes two analyses and some careful observation skills to discover a wizard, but when you do, it is a powerful number to play. You will be working with best number and overdue analyses, and running a filter to get your wizards.

The **wizard** is a number that was hot early and disappeared late, that is, ran cold. If, on the surface, it looks like you will be running long-term and short-terms filters, you got it right. You will be aiming for different data from each analysis and will combine the results for a powerful group of numbers. You are looking for established long-term hot numbers that have become overdue.

The mystical wizard has established long-term strength, so it is a number you expect to come back from its cold spell and fulfill its early magic by getting hot again.

Here's how you discover wizards:

You start by running it solid with a Best Number Analysis of 100 games to isolate the 10 hottest numbers. You then run an Overdue Number Analysis of the previous 25 games and isolate the 10 coldest numbers. You compare the results of both analyses. When numbers coincide between the two analyses, you have found a wizard.

You treat wizards as major keys, making sure they are treated as the most important numbers among your chosen numbers and playing them accordingly in most of your tickets. However, if the wizard is very powerful—that is, if it ranks among the top five hot numbers in a 100 game best number analysis and also among the top five overdue numbers in a 25 game overdue analysis—you have a **high wizard** and you can play it as a master key, covering the high wizard on every ticket you play.

WIZARDS & HIGH WIZARDS

	Wizard	High Wizard
Regression Best Number	100 games	100 games
Regression Overdue	25 games	25 games
Hot & Cold Rank	Top 10	Top 5
Type of Key	Major	Master

KEY NUMBERS SUMMARY

I have covered a lot of ground in this chapter, including important keys such as best (hot) numbers and overdue (cold) numbers, as well as master, major, minor and third keys. I've also examined the various types of lucky numbers that can be combined or used as keys, plus wizards and high wizards, and how you might use all these keys with your chosen numbers to form powerful tickets.

The keys will slot right into your core strategies. Your basic decision will be to determine how many numbers you want to use; what confidence levels, if any, you want to assign to your pool of numbers; what core strategy you will use to attack lottery and lotto games; whether to add lucky numbers; and ultimately, how many tickets you want to play while chasing the big jackpot.

Okay, time to step forward again.

SECTION III

WHEELS

9

WHEELING STRATEGY

If you were to choose every number you identified as a potential winner, the end result would be an unwieldy number of tickets played—in other words, you'd spend way too much money on lottery tickets! Few players want to put out that much money on lottery and lotto games and frankly, it would be a bad idea to gamble away huge chunks of money on a game where the odds are so long.

The idea is to manage your chosen and key numbers in a system so that if they come up, you have an excellent chance of winning prizes—and to cover your important numbers without spending a ridiculous amount of money. In other words, you want good coverage of your numbers at a reasonable cost.

That is where *wheeling systems*, or *wheels*, come into play.

THE VALUE OF WHEELS

A **lottery wheel**, or simply a **wheel** (or **wheeling system**), is a system of strategically distributing chosen numbers that gives a player partial coverage of all possible combinations such that a group of tickets can be played at a reasonable cost, that is, much less than if every combination were played. Technically, I am referring to an **abbreviated wheeling system**, but for ease of discussion, I will stick with the simple term "wheel" to indicate strategically constructed combinations of numbers and use the term **full wheel** to describe the type of wheel where every single combination is covered.

For example, if you're playing a six-ball game and have 10 numbers you want to play, a wheel would create various combinations of the tickets so that if your numbers hit, many winning possibilities would be covered.

Wheeling allows you to take a chosen set of numbers and combine them to improve your odds of winning prizes if enough of your chosen numbers get drawn. Wheels provide a wide coverage of your chosen numbers without your having to play every combination. Obviously, the more combinations you cover, the greater the expense to play your numbers, but you don't want to break the bank if you have, say, 11 or 12 numbers. The idea of the wheeling systems is to reduce that risk while still giving you an efficient coverage of your chosen numbers.

With luck, you may win several prizes from your set of numbers. If you're very lucky, you may win the big jackpot.

You can use as many numbers in your wheels as you want; however, an individual number is used only one time per wheeling system. For example, if you've chosen the following nine numbers—7, 13, 22, 23, 24, 28, 41, 42, and 49—you would choose a wheeling system to distribute them to the number of tickets you elect to play. For example, a ticket wouldn't have the number 41 twice, or any other number twice for that matter, because a number cannot be drawn twice in a lotto game.

THE COST OF PLAYING EVERY CHOSEN NUMBER

You must select a minimum of six numbers in a six-ball game (or five numbers in a five-ball game) to be able to play a ticket. When you select exactly six numbers to work with, your bets are easy. There is only one possible combination of those six numbers. You would be playing a full wheel. Again, in lotto as opposed to lottery games, it makes no difference in what order the numbers get chosen. If the six numbers you picked are drawn, you're a winner.

The complications occur when you want to play a much wider spread of numbers than the minimum six-number ticket to have every possible combination covered. For example, if you choose seven numbers, you'd need seven tickets to cover all possible combinations and have a full wheel. At $1 per ticket, an investment of $7 is not overwhelming. But what if you choose a far greater pool of numbers than seven and want to cover a full wheel?

Before I address that, let's see how the tickets get formed if you play a full wheel of seven chosen numbers and then a full wheel of eight chosen numbers. In this first example, you choose seven numbers to play and have exactly seven possible combinations. That is six more combinations than if you played just one ticket.

To organize wheels and easily disperse your numbers, you set up a *wheel template*. A **wheel template** matches letters of a wheeling system with chosen numbers so that you can create wheels with good coverage of the numbers you'll be playing. You start, however, with a **letter conversion chart,** which assigns one letter to each chosen number so that the chosen numbers can be correctly inserted into a wheel template. For example, if you were using ten chosen numbers in a wheel, you would use the first ten letters of the alphabet, thus: A, B, C, D, E, F, G, H, I and J. In the example below, we're using seven numbers, so just the letters A though G are needed.

Since our analysis gave us seven chosen numbers to play—1, 13, 22, 27, 32, 46, 48—we'll match them up with the letters. You set up a letter conversion chart.

Let's have a look.

LETTER CONVERSION CHART

A	**B**	**C**	**D**	**E**	**F**	**G**
1	13	22	27	32	46	48

Each letter represents a position on the wheel and the numbers below the letter represents your chosen numbers. When you create a wheel, you replace the letters in the wheel with the numbers below them in the conversion table to create the tickets you're going to play.

The actual wheel is a matrix with the letters in position ready to be replaced by numbers. Here is a wheel template for seven chosen numbers and seven games.

WHEEL TEMPLATE
7 Chosen Numbers / 7 Tickets / 0 Keys

1.	A	B	C	D	E	F
2.	A	B	C	D	E	G
3.	A	B	C	D	F	G
4.	A	B	C	E	F	G
5.	A	B	D	E	F	G
6.	A	C	D	E	F	G
7.	B	C	D	E	F	G

You replace every letter symbol with the chosen number that corresponds to it. For example, the letter A gets replaced with 1, and the letter B with 13. The chart below has replaced all the letters with the corresponding numbers from the wheel template to show the final tickets you'll be playing.

LEVEL I WHEEL					
7 Chosen Numbers / 7 Tickets / 0 Keys					
1. 1	13	22	27	32	46
2. 1	13	22	27	32	48
3. 1	13	22	27	46	48
4. 1	13	22	32	46	48
5. 1	13	27	32	46	48
6. 1	22	27	32	46	48
7. 13	22	27	32	46	48

PLAYING AN 8TH NUMBER

What if you add another number, an eighth, and want to play all combinations? This time you add the number 49 to your mix. You would have to buy 28 tickets to cover all the possibilities of a full wheel, 21 more possibilities than your pool of seven numbers.

Here is how that would look.

Chosen Numbers: 1, 13, 22, 27, 32, 46, 48, 49

Following is a letter conversion chart that would correspond to your chosen numbers. Any set of chosen numbers could be plugged into this wheel template, or any other wheel template if you were to play the same number of games. You're going to use the above eight numbers since these are your chosen numbers. Eight chosen numbers requires eight letters, one for each number, so we work with the letters A through H.

LETTER CONVERSION CHART

<u>A</u>	<u>B</u>	<u>C</u>	<u>D</u>	<u>E</u>	<u>F</u>	<u>G</u>	<u>H</u>
1	13	22	27	32	46	48	49

Your wheeling template is below. It shows every possible combination for those eight chosen numbers, a total of 28 tickets.

WHEEL TEMPLATE
8 Chosen Numbers / 28 Tickets / 0 Keys

1.	A	B	C	D	E	F
2.	A	B	C	D	E	G
3.	A	B	C	D	E	H
4.	A	B	C	D	F	G
5.	A	B	C	D	F	H
6.	A	B	C	D	G	H
7.	A	B	C	E	F	G
8.	A	B	C	E	F	H
9.	A	B	C	E	G	H
10.	A	B	C	F	G	H
11.	A	B	D	E	F	G
12.	A	B	D	E	F	H
13.	A	B	D	E	G	H
14.	A	B	D	F	G	H
15.	A	B	E	F	G	H
16.	A	C	D	E	F	G
17.	A	C	D	E	F	H
18.	A	C	D	E	G	H
19.	A	C	D	F	G	H
20.	A	C	E	F	G	H
21.	A	D	E	F	G	H
22.	B	C	D	E	F	G
23.	B	C	D	E	F	H
24.	B	C	D	E	G	H
25.	B	C	D	F	G	H
26.	B	C	E	F	G	H
27.	B	D	E	F	G	H
28.	C	D	E	F	G	H

Replacing the letters with your chosen numbers, you get the following 28 ticket combinations ready to play:

LEVEL I WHEEL
8 Chosen Numbers / 28 Tickets / 0 Keys

1.	1	13	22	27	32	46
2.	1	13	22	27	32	48
3.	1	13	22	27	32	49
4.	1	13	22	27	46	48
5.	1	13	22	27	46	49
6.	1	13	22	27	48	49
7.	1	13	22	32	46	48
8.	1	13	22	32	46	49
9.	1	13	22	32	48	49
10.	1	13	22	46	48	49
11.	1	13	27	32	46	48
12.	1	13	27	32	46	49
13.	1	13	27	32	48	49
14.	1.	22	27	46	48	49
15.	1.	22	32	46	48	49
16.	1.	22	27	32	46	48
17.	1.	22	27	32	46	49
18.	1	22	27	32	48	49
19.	1	22	27	46	48	49
20.	1	22	32	46	48	49
21.	1	27	32	46	48	49
22.	13	22	27	32	46	48
23.	13	22	27	32	46	49
24.	13	22	27	32	48	49
25.	13	22	27	46	48	49
26.	13	22	32	46	48	49
27.	13	27	32	46	48	49
28.	22	27	32	46	48	49

This wheel covers every possible combination of eight numbers in a six-ball lotto, a total of 28 possible combinations. You can see how the number of tickets you need for full coverage gets exponentially larger each time a chosen number is added to the mix.

Let's say you wanted to play 10 numbers in every combination possible for a full wheel, adding two more chosen numbers to your pool. You would have to play 210 combinations just to cover them all. At $1 per ticket, that would cost you $210. That's way too much money, especially if you're a regular player. If you did this two times per week, you would be playing tickets at a rate of over $20,000 per year. That's a lot of money, a ridiculous amount to be spending on lottery tickets.

What if you add another number or play one fewer number and want to play all combinations? The following chart shows you the number of six-ball tickets you would need to cover every chosen number in your pool and have a full wheel.

COMBINATIONS NEEDED FOR A FULL WHEEL

Numbers Chosen	All Combinations
6	6
7	7
8	28
9	84
10	210
11	462
12	924
13	1,716
14	3,003
15	5,005
16	8,008
17	12,376
18	18,564
19	27,132
20	38,760
21	54,264
22	74,613
23	100,947
24	134,596
25	177,100

As you choose more numbers, the tickets you need to cover all the winning possibilities of a full wheel get exponentially and crazily higher. Every possible combination in a full wheel of 25 numbers would cost you $177,100. You have to be crazy, foolish or something else to wager that kind of money on a lotto game.

One more number added the original pool of 12 numbers that I spoke about earlier means that you would have to buy 1,716 tickets for a full wheel. At $1 per ticket, that would be $1,716 worth of tickets for just one drawing! That's way too much unless you're the most serious of players or have a very serious plan that makes mathematical sense—in other words, you've found an exposable flaw in the game—or unless you just have money to burn.

The idea of lottery and lotto games is to win a lot of money from a *small* investment, for many people $1, for some as much as $10 or $20, or perhaps $40 per play for super-aggressive players that can afford it.

But $1,716 worth of tickets?

Luckily for you, there is a way to cover a large group of numbers without buying a basket of tickets. The secret, as many serious lottery and lotto players have learned, is to combine your numbers into groups of tickets such that all your numbers are in play—but at a fraction of the cost.

We'll examine these efficient and powerful wheels as part of our next discussion.

WHEELS & KEY NUMBERS

Combining key numbers with wheels is the basis of many of the Level III strategies. A master key number, as I discussed earlier in chapter 8, *Level II Strategies: Key Numbers,* gets used in every wheel that gets formed and is either a user-designated number or is derived from one of our analyses. In that chapter I discussed other types of key numbers as well—major keys, minor keys and third keys.

To bring out the full power of the various types of keys requires prudent use of wheels for full coverage of chosen numbers and keys and for efficiency in making tickets.

We'll look at this topic and more in this important chapter.

USING KEY NUMBERS IN WHEELS

Let's say you have identified 11 chosen numbers to populate your tickets—the 1, 3, 11, 13, 19, 29, 30, 33, 37, 38 and 39. You start by setting up a letter conversion chart.

LETTER CONVERSION CHART

A	B	C	D	E	F	G	H	I	J	K
1	3	11	13	19	29	30	33	37	38	39

In a Level I wheel, you will be dividing these chosen numbers almost equally among your tickets. You can't cover a full wheel without buying a boatload of tickets (in this instance, 462 tickets) so you wheel the numbers, or at least spread the numbers around. Your budget is $10 so you have 10 tickets to work with and you want to play 11 numbers. You may end up with each number being played five or six times each among 10 tickets.

Following is a wheel template I created for 11 chosen numbers and ten tickets.

WHEEL TEMPLATE					
11 Chosen Numbers / 10 Tickets / 0 Keys					
1. A	B	C	D	E	F
2. A	B	D	E	F	K
3. A	C	D	F	G	H
4. A	C	F	H	I	J
5. A	D	E	F	G	K
6. A	E	G	H	I	J
7. B	E	H	I	J	K
8. B	C	D	E	H	K
9. B	C	D	G	I	J
10. B	C	G	I	J	K

Here's what your tickets would look like after you substitute the chosen numbers for the letters in the template:

LEVEL I WHEEL
11 Chosen Numbers / 10 Tickets / 0 Keys

1.	1	3	11	13	19	29
2.	1	3	13	19	29	39
3.	1	11	13	29	30	33
4.	1	11	29	33	37	38
5.	1	13	19	29	30	39
6.	1	19	30	33	37	38
7.	3	19	33	37	38	39
8.	3	11	13	19	33	39
9.	3	11	13	30	37	38
10.	3	11	30	37	38	39

The 10 tickets are displayed with the numbers from left to right. The first ticket contains the numbers 1, 3, 11, 13, 19 and 29, and the second ticket contains the numbers 1, 3, 13, 19, 29 and 39, and so on down to the tenth ticket, which has the numbers 3, 11, 30, 37, 38 and 39.

These numbers appear on the following number of tickets:

FREQUENCY OF USE CHART
Level I Wheel

1	3	11	13	19	29
6	6	6	6	6	5

30	33	37	38	39
5	5	5	5	5

The 10 tickets illustrate a standard Level I wheel using our core strategies. But through advanced analysis of Level II strategies, you have decided to work with keys. You have designated two keys, one a major key that will appear on eight tickets, and the second a minor key, which will appear on seven tickets. These keys could be kings or queens, they could be wizards or lucky numbers, or they could be derived from any type of analysis you use to pull the keys.

We have designated the "**1**" as the major key, which is represented by the letter "A" in our template, and the "**13**" as the minor key, represented by the letter "D." Let's redo the tickets to take advantage of weighting our best numbers, that is, using keys, and see how that would change the tickets.

First, the template of the very same numbers again.

LETTER CONVERSION CHART

A	B	C	D	E	F	G	H	I	J	K
1	3	11	13	19	29	30	33	37	38	39

Here is a wheel template that has been set up for 11 chosen numbers and 10 tickets. The keys, "A" and "D" are highlighted in bold text so you can easily see how they play into the tickets.

WHEEL TEMPLATE
11 Chosen Numbers / 10 Tickets / 2 Keys

1.	A	B	C	**D**	E	F
2.	A	B	**D**	E	F	K
3.	A	B	**D**	F	G	H
4.	A	C	F	H	I	J
5.	A	**D**	E	F	G	K
6.	A	B	**D**	H	I	J
7.	E	G	H	I	J	K
8.	A	C	**D**	E	H	K
9.	A	C	**D**	G	I	J
10.	B	C	G	I	J	K

Below is what this new set of tickets, featuring a major key and a minor key, would look like. The keys, "**A**" and "**B**," which will be replaced by the chosen numbers "1" and "13" respectively, are highlighted in bold text so you can easily see how they play into the tickets.

LEVEL II WHEEL
11 Chosen Numbers / 10 Tickets / 2 Keys

1.	1	3	11	**13**	19	29
2.	1	3	**13**	19	29	39
3.	1	3	**13**	29	30	33
4.	1	11	29	33	37	38
5.	1	**13**	19	29	30	39
6.	1	3	**13**	33	37	38
7.	19	30	33	37	38	39
8.	1	11	**13**	19	33	39
9.	1	11	**13**	30	37	38
10.	3	11	30	37	38	39

FREQUENCY OF USE CHART					
Level II Wheel					
1	**3**	**11**	**13**	**19**	**29**
8	5	5	7	5	5
30	**33**	**37**	**38**	**39**	
5	5	5	5	5	

Each of your chosen numbers appears on five of the 10 tickets, with the exception of your major key, the 1, which plays on eight tickets and your minor key, the 13, which plays on seven tickets. You could place even more emphasis on your major key by using it on all tickets—that is, giving it a higher confidence level—and making it a master key. To do this you would have to tone down the frequency of your other chosen numbers to make this adjustment, or downgrade the minor key (the 13 represented by the letter "D") to a standard chosen number to make more room for the master number on the tickets that currently lack it.

The amount of confidence you place on certain numbers is a discipline and discussion in itself, but to keep your strategies manageable, look at it like this: If you are elevating strategies to a Level II status by designating one or more keys, just ascertain whether you want a full master played on all tickets, or simply a major key that is pushed harder than the other numbers but does not offer full coverage.

Of course, you would use the strength of a key's previous performance and the criteria of a Level III strategy to help you determine the confidence level you have in a key, and whether you would promote it to a master key or simply play it as a major key.

COVERING MORE TICKETS

The more tickets you buy, the greater coverage you will have with your chosen numbers and, of course, the greater strength you'll be giving to key numbers. The number of tickets you decide to play has to keep a balance between how much you can or should spend on buying lottery and lotto tickets, and how much coverage you would like to get with your chosen and key numbers.

But again, money management must always be the boss in any form of gambling. And yes, my friends, lottery and lotto games are as much gambling as anything you might do in a casino or bingo parlor, so how many tickets you play, meaning how much money you spend playing them, is a very important consideration in your plans.

Just be smart.

USING STRATEGY PROFILES

To best organize your plays, I find it helpful to create a *strategy profile*. A **strategy profile** shows the basic information you'll use to form a wheel, including the game played, type or types of strategies being used, the pool of chosen numbers, the keys used, and the number of tickets being purchased. With a strategy profile by your side, you get a clear look at how you're attacking a game and can keep an organized history of your results in a book. This will allow you to tinker with and improve your strategies.

Here is an example of a strategy profile

STRATEGY PROFILE

Game	Six-Ball Lotto
Strategy	Best Number Analysis
Regression Level	100 Games
Number of Tickets	7
Total Pool of Numbers	10
Chosen Numbers	8
40, 12, 11, 2, 21, 35, 32, 48	
Keys	2
41, 8	

CREATING A WHEEL

In the 7-ticket, 10-number and 2-key wheel template described in the strategy profile and shown below, greater confidence is given to positions A and B (the actual numbers for these positions are 41 and 8) and less confidence to the other chosen numbers. In other words, the wheel has two keys, a master and a minor key, along with the pool of chosen numbers. The keys are highlighted in bold.

First, your letter conversion chart. Since there are 10 chosen numbers, you use 10 letters, A through J.

LETTER CONVERSION CHART

A	**B**	**C**	**D**	**E**	**F**	**G**	**H**	**I**	**J**
41	**8**	40	12	11	2	21	35	32	48

Now the wheel template.

WHEEL TEMPLATE
10 Chosen Numbers / 7 Tickets / 2 Keys

1.	A	B	C	D	E	J
2.	A	B	C	D	F	H
3.	A	B	C	D	I	J
4.	A	B	D	E	F	G
5.	A	B	F	G	H	I
6.	A	C	E	F	G	H
7.	A	E	G	H	I	J

Each row represents a ticket with the six numbers chosen for that ticket. Here is the frequency of positions used in your wheel, with each letter representing an actual number that will replace it so you clearly see the tickets you will be playing.

FREQUENCY OF POSITION CHART
Level II Wheel

Letter	Frequency
A	7 (all tickets)
B	5
C	4
D	4
E	4
F	4
G	4
H	4
I	4
J	3

Your most important number, in the A position, appears seven times; your second most important number, in the B position, appears five times; and the rest of the numbers appear on four tickets or on three tickets. This wheel gives you complete coverage of your most important number, the "A" position, which appears on all tickets, plus broad coverage of your other chosen numbers.

You plug your numbers in, replacing its letter with its corresponding chosen number, to see what actual tickets get formed. You use the wheel template shown earlier to guide you in the number replacement. These are the tickets created by the 7-ticket, 10-number, 2-key wheel:

LEVEL II WHEEL
10 Chosen Numbers / 7 Tickets / 2 Keys

1.	41	8	40	12	11	48
2.	41	8	40	12	2	35
3.	41	8	40	12	32	48
4.	41	8	12	11	2	21
5.	41	8	2	21	35	32
6.	41	40	11	2	21	35
7.	41	11	21	35	32	48

REFINING A WHEEL

To refine a wheel with new parameters, you would adjust some of the input factors; for example, give greater importance to a third number. Let's take these same numbers and create a wheel for 11 games instead of seven. You will now give a third number prominence in your tickets, that is, you will play a third key. That number is 40, which is in the C position. Let's make a strategy profile first.

STRATEGY PROFILE

Game	6-Ball Lotto
Strategy	Best Number Analysis
Regression Level	100 Games
Number of Tickets	11
Total Pool of Numbers	10
Chosen Numbers	7
12, 11, 2, 21, 35, 32, 48	
Keys	3
41, 8, 40	

WHEEL TEMPLATE
10 Chosen Numbers / 11 Tickets / 3 Keys

1.	A	B	C	D	E	F
2.	A	B	C	D	H	I
3.	A	B	C	E	F	G
4.	A	B	C	E	H	I
5.	A	B	C	F	G	J
6.	A	B	C	F	H	I
7.	A	B	C	G	I	J
8.	A	B	C	H	I	J
9.	A	B	D	E	G	H
10.	A	D	E	F	G	J
11.	A	D	F	H	I	J

The A-B-C positions have been designated as the most important, with the A position having the very highest confidence of all the positions. In fact, it is played as a master key. Here is the frequency of positions used in this specialized 11-ticket, 10-number, 3-key wheel:

FREQUENCY OF POSITION CHART
Level II Wheel

Letter	Frequency
A	11 (all tickets)
B	9
C	8
D	5
E	5
F	6
G	5
H	6
I	6
J	5

Here again is the letter conversions chart showing the numbers by position:

LETTER CONVERSION CHART

A	B	C	D	E	F	G	H	I	J
41	8	40	12	11	2	21	35	32	48

Now insert the numbers.

LEVEL II WHEEL
10 Chosen Numbers / 11 Tickets / 3 Keys

1.	41	8	40	12	11	2
2.	41	8	40	12	35	32
3.	41	8	40	11	2	21
4.	41	8	40	11	35	32
5.	41	8	40	2	21	48
6.	41	8	40	2	35	32
7.	41	8	40	21	32	48
8.	41	8	40	35	32	48
9.	41	8	12	11	21	35
10.	41	12	11	2	21	48
11.	41	12	2	35	32	48

These are the tickets that have been wheeled for your 11-ticket lottery game.

WHEEL REVIEW

We've created a number of wheels in this chapter, showing various numbers, tickets and keys being played. These are some of the endless examples of wheels that can be created with a vast array of numbers, games and keys.

It is beyond the scope of this book to show a full range of wheels—which would be an enormous task in itself—but you have several options if you want to put a strong line of wheels into your arsenal. You are advised to buy Prof. Jones wheel packages at cardozabooks.com or from the ads in the back of this book, or use www.lotterysupersystem.com, which automatically creates powerful wheels for you according to parameters that you set.

UNDERWHEELING & OVERWHEELING

It would be frustrating to book a winner with four out of the six numbers chosen in a drawing and think you were so close to choosing the fifth or even the sixth winning number! Sure, you're happy with a winning ticket but you're thinking, "If only I had played that extra number or the extra ticket that I was just about to buy."

Playing fewer tickets than warranted based on a group of strong chosen numbers is called **underwheeling**. While it's hard to know exactly how many tickets you should play given the strength of the numbers that your analyses identify, at the same time, you never know which numbers will hit. You'll have heartbreaking near misses—after the fact, of course—and stare in disbelief at an almost-win.

That's where more tickets come into play. More tickets and more numbers covered give you better chances—that's straight math—but you must always keep the number of tickets reasonable for what you can afford to spend, both financially and emotionally. Again, I refer you to plain old common sense and the *money management* section later in this book.

Overwheeling means playing too many tickets on good numbers in a wheel; in other words, spending too much money on lottery and lotto games. Overwheeling is way too dangerous, which is why all discussions start with money management—what you can afford to spend on a financial and emotional level—and continue on from there. You can't let the possibilities of winning and the excitement of the near misses in a week make you dizzy, because if you get too dizzy, your bankroll could disappear. And that's not a good thing.

The middle ground of how many tickets you should play is a question that only you can answer. You just have to find the middle ground between overwheeling and underwheeling.

BIG WHEEL STRATEGY: INCREASING YOUR ODDS BY 10-50 TIMES—OR MORE!

Let's not fool ourselves. Despite our powerful strategies, jackpots are extremely hard to hit. The odds are so astronomical that you need all the help you can get to hit the big prize. We've shown you how to identify patterns and play important numbers and wheel them into an effective array of tickets. You can cover a maximum amount of bases with a minimum amount of investment, yet still, there are a lot of numbers out there.

But you can increase your umbrella of coverage to 10, 20 and even 50 times of what you are currently covering—and it won't cost you a dime. Nothing.

All you have to do is run a *big wheel*. A **big wheel** is a pool of multiple players acting together as a syndicate, sharing tickets and sharing wins. It is a powerful strategy for attacking jackpots, and even more powerful when you're working together with a cohesive strategy. Let's say you get 10 family members together and each of you contributes $10 to the pool, with each dollar representing one ticket. Now you have 100 tickets in the big wheel, a far more powerful umbrella than if you had worked the numbers alone, especially if you coordinate the approach and use the strategies outlined in this book.

What if you get 20 coworkers together with the same premise?

Now your big wheel syndicate controls 200 tickets, a much more formidable front than just the 10 tickets you were going to play on your own.

The more numbers you have in play, or looking at it another way, the more tickets you have in the raffle, the greater your chances of winning.

Put together a pool of family, friends, fellow workers, club members—any group that has a common bond—and pool your resources. Have each person in the pool contribute an equal amount of money and pick an equal number of tickets. Write all the names on a piece of paper, plus a few lines stating who is in the pool and what tickets are covered, so that there is no misunderstanding later in case one of the tickets comes home with all the gold.

The agreement can either state that all members of the pool split the prize equally, which is the best and cleanest way, or you could add the proviso that the person who actually picked the winning ticket gets a 5% bonus off the top, with the rest of the jackpot split equally among all the contributors.

The big wheel strategy has proven successful many times and is a fun way to play. Now your team is working together as a unit. So what if you split the money? If the prize pool is $300 million and 20 of you have to split it, is anyone really complaining? There's plenty of money to go around, like $15 million each! You can be the first one with the largesse. Take everyone out to dinner at a fancy restaurant. Peel off the tiniest micro fraction from your pile of cash and foot the bill.

You have so much money it won't even make a dent.

In 1998 a group of 13 workers in Ohio pooled their tickets and won over $161 million ($161,496,959.30). As that pool got bigger and bigger, these workers formed a coalition to attack the jackpot. And they got there. That's more than $12 million per player! In 2013, a group of 16 garage workers claimed one of the three winning tickets in a Powerball jackpot of $488 million—the group sharing a prize of about $160 million. There are many more stories like this one. How about this group from Spain who claimed the world's largest jackpot prize as of early 2016?

In 2012 a whopping $950 million (almost $1 billion) was won by a syndicate of 180 players. That's well more than $50 million per player—plenty to go around for everyone.

Maybe your syndicate will be the next group to win several hundred million—or be the first to actually win $1 billion!

WHEEL NUMBER DISTRIBUTION

You have seen how a wheel might distribute numbers throughout the ticket. When a number is earmarked as very important, it gets placement on all tickets, while other numbers that are important but are not considered super elite, get good placement, but not the highest confidence given to the top one. As you become a more advanced player and learn more tools of analysis, isolation, keys and advanced strategies, you will learn how to identify and adjust the importance of certain numbers in your wheel so that you get the right balance of aggressiveness in your high confidence numbers.

Think of each chosen number as an independent lever that you push up for more gas or ease up on for less gas. Give it more gas and the number will be more aggressively placed among your tickets; give it less gas and the number will be pulled back on some tickets in favor of other numbers, though it will still be in play.

With good numbers and good wheels, you can attack lottery and lotto draws with authority. And maybe, just maybe, your numbers will come good for you!

SECTION IV

ADVANCED STRATEGIES

11

THREE & FOUR-BALL LEVEL III LOTTERY STRATEGIES

In the *Level I Play: The Core Strategies* chapter, you learned how to run a positional analysis for lottery games. Now you're going to go one step further and learn how to enhance those strategies. With the positional analysis as your foundation, you will look for the sub-analyses that best suit your philosophy—hot numbers, cold numbers, clusters and other strategies—to obtain the optimal numbers you'll use to form your tickets. Then you'll take that one step further by adding Level II keys and combining all this power into advanced Level III play.

Let's review a few basics.

In three-ball and four-ball lottery games, the order in which numbers are drawn is important because payouts are only made for correctly chosen numbers in the *exact* order in which they were drawn. So you want to diligently chart the drawn balls in the proper position. *Positional analysis* will be at the heart of your winning strategies and you will use this analysis to extract a best numbers analysis, cold-number analysis, and other bread-and-butter strategies.

PLAYING A SINGLE TICKET

Let's say you ran a positional analysis of the last 100 drawings in a three-ball lottery game and organized the data into a Best Number Analysis. These were the results:

BEST NUMBER ANALYSIS
Three-Ball Lottery / 100 Drawings

Position 1		Position 2		Position 3		
#	Frq	#	Frq	#	Frq	Best Numbers
7	19	0	16	2	15	Most Draws
6	17	3	15	4	15	Second
0	16	9	15	8	15	Third

Let's see what you can do with these results.

In the above sample for a three-ball game, you see that number 7 (19 times) was the most popular number in the first column, 0 (16 times) was the most popular in the second column, and 2 (15 times) led the field in the third column.

You would display your top numbers as shown:

7-0-2

If you were running a Best Number Analysis, it would display this ticket as your top result over the previous 100 games. If you were playing just one ticket, the 7-0-2 would be your combination to play. Even though the 6 in the first column was the second most frequently drawn digit of all numbers drawn, it is not one of your top three numbers because the three-ball game (and the four-ball game as well) is analyzed by position. The top performing numbers from each of the lottery bins are

automatically going to be the three best numbers to play—
they have already proven themselves in the field of battle.

You choose the 7 because you are searching for bias or a hot
number, and the first column is a separate drawing from the
other two columns. If you were playing the minimum number
of tickets—which means you would play only your top number in each column—that 6 in the first column wouldn't make
the cut.

Note also that in the third column, the numbers 2, 4 and 8 all
were drawn 15 times. Why did we choose the 2-ball over the
4-ball and 8-ball? We elected to use the number 2 because it
was the most recent number to get to 15 selections. To determine this last ball drawn of the three candidates, you have to
do a little forensic research and look at the results from the last
group of drawings. You see this:

100th	9	4	2
99th	0	1	9
98th	0	3	2
97th	8	0	3
96th	6	7	6

On the 100th drawing, the 2-ball was picked, so you take that
as your best and hottest number of the three positions. Your
selection is reinforced by two other factors:

1. The 2-ball was drawn in third position on two of the
   past three drawings. For a Best Number Analysis, that
   certainly says "hot" because it is trending as well.
2. Neither the 4-ball nor the 8-ball was drawn in the prior
   five drawings.

But what if you thought these last five drawings (or even the last 10 drawings) showed such a significant current trend that you needed to factor those results into your analysis and resultant tickets? That would be a keen observation. It's a high level play to mix short and long term trends to maximum efficiency. A set of very advanced plays is used by an allegiance of serious players who specifically focus on decade trends, long and short Level III strategies, and wizards to carve out winnings. You get a slight taste of that thinking here.

In the above analysis, where the 2, 4 and 8 balls were each drawn 15 times over the last 100 games, you could have chosen the 4-ball over the 2-ball because it was the first number to reach 15 picks. That is a criterion that you'll often use to choose among ties. But when you're playing hot, you often want to stick to a *hot-hot number*. A **hot-hot number** is a chosen number or a key that was the most *recently* drawn (as opposed to the first drawn) when compared to other hot numbers.

You could also choose a **hot-five number**—a number that has been hot compared to other hot numbers—over the most recent period of five drawings

In this case, since you're playing just one ticket, you only want the three best numbers, so you stick with the hot-hot number for the tiebreaker in the third position.

PLAYING MULTIPLE TICKETS

We have discussed how you arrive at the numbers you'll play if you were just playing a single ticket. But what if you were playing more than one ticket? Then, of course, you would need more than three numbers to play.

So how do you go about getting more chosen numbers?

The process is easy because you have already done the work. Your positional analysis has identified the best-performing numbers, so you just have to decide how many of those numbers—and what criteria—you will use. For example, do you want to use the best numbers in the first two spots on all three positions? Do you want to use only the very best numbers regardless of position, which could mean that you take, for example, one number from Position 1 and one from Position 2 and three from Position 3?

You could use all the ties if they are your best numbers or use the best number in a group of ties according to criteria I outlined earlier. There are many possibilities on how to play your selections.

And then, how many tickets?

These are decisions only you can make. You have to decide on your philosophical winning approach and run with it. When playing hot, you might want to give preference to recently drawn numbers among your chosen numbers by going with hot-hot numbers or hot-five numbers. Similarly, when playing overdue numbers, you could give preference to **cold-cold numbers**, chosen numbers or keys that haven't been drawn in the longest span of games (as opposed to most recently drawn), compared to other overdue numbers, or a **cold-10 number**—a number that has been cold compared to other overdue numbers—over the most recent period of 10 drawings.

Because of the greater scarcity of cold numbers compared to hot numbers, you want a sampling of at least 10 games when analyzing overdue numbers to avoid the inevitable ties of too small a sample.

I am loading you up on powerful lottery and lotto strategies so that you will have a full arsenal to attack the game. The approach that is best for you is one that you will have to decide.

Let's look further into the issue of expanding your pool of chosen numbers so that you can have greater coverage and play more tickets.

SELECTING MORE CHOSEN NUMBERS

We'll borrow a theoretical computer interface—I promise I'll make it easy—because it is instructive in the process of picking best numbers. Below is what a computer interface might look like when you go about selecting your chosen numbers. You can see how the thinking might work for you..

BEST NUMBERS: INSTRUCTIVE INTERFACE

AUTOMATIC BEST NUMBER FUNCTION
Select Number of Balls by Position

Position 1	Position 2	Position 3
1-3	1-3	1-3

Position 1		Position 2		Position 3		
#	Frq	#	Frq	#	Frq	Best Numbers
7	19	0	16	2	15	Most Draws
6	17	3	15	4	15	Second
0	16	9	15	8	15	Third

On this interface, you have chosen to activate three positions (since you are analyzing a three-ball game) and play the positions aggressively. You decide to play the top three balls in each position. Under Position 1, the "1-3" indicates that you are playing the top three balls in that position as selected by the analysis method you are using. (It does not reference the balls numbered 1 through 3, just their status in terms of top-performing balls.)

You could also set your parameters to choose four balls in the first position and two balls each for Positions 2 and 3. That setting would look like this:

AUTOMATIC BEST NUMBER FUNCTION		
Select Number of Balls by Position		
Position 1	**Position 2**	**Position 3**
1-4	1-2	1-2

You would choose a total of eight numbers with this setting, down from nine balls in the first setting, only this time you frontload four balls from the first position and two each from the latter two positions. Since each position represents a unique pool of 10 balls, represented here by columns, there could be duplicates across the columns.

For example, your chosen numbers could look like this:

Position 1	**Position 2**	**Position 3**
0, 5, 6	0, 7	7, 9

You choose the numbers to be selected depending upon the strategy you're implementing. If it were hot numbers, you would take the best performing ones for the regression level chosen, let's say, a 100-game regression level. Or, for example, if you were running an Overdue Number Analysis, you might choose from the coldest numbers, banking on the theory that those numbers are due to be drawn.

AUTOMATIC CHOSEN NUMBERS

In a specialized online software package such as lotterysupersystem.com, your top-performing numbers, that is, your chosen numbers, would automatically be generated according to the criteria you selected, and you would have the opportunity to add confidence levels and key numbers (if desired) to make powerful tickets.

If you were analyzing a four-ball game instead of a three-ball game, you would activate Position 4 as well and everything else would be figured in the exact manner as I have shown. You would choose a Level I strategy and select chosen numbers position by position according to the strength of your results, the number of balls you want represented on your ticket, and the number of tickets you want to play.

TAKING IT TO LEVEL II

Level II strategies consist of identifying keys, which I talked about in depth in chapter 8, *Level II Strategies: Key Numbers*. To short-circuit this discussion so that you can get right to the Level III strategies, we'll jump forward and make advanced tickets ready for betting, assuming that you fully understand the premises and workings of extracting keys.

TAKING IT TO LEVEL III

The Level III strategies bring in keys to make your tickets more complex and more powerful. As discussed, all numbers are not the same. That's why you have chosen numbers and that's why you have a vast pool of numbers you don't play at all. But even among the chosen numbers, again, all numbers are not the same. Some are more valuable than others and you're going to take that into account.

Earlier we discussed making the powerful Level I plays from your chosen numbers, but we didn't push our more powerful numbers—every chosen number was treated the same. Now we're going to amp that up.

In the three-ball lottery example earlier, we discovered that the numbers 7, 6 and 0 were the most frequently drawn in the first position, so we chart that as follows:

FIRST POSITION RESULTS	
1st Ball	**Frequency**
7	19
6	17
0	16

But you need more chosen numbers to attack the lottery more aggressively. Also, you have two more positions to fill up with at least one ball each. We're going to expand the look at our best numbers over a 100-game regression analysis showing all three positions in the three-ball game.

This time we've shown the top five performing numbers, though in reality we're only going to play the top one, two or three of them. Betting five numbers in three columns is way too aggressive. It would be too costly to cover so many numbers. Instead, you would like to restrict your bets to the very best numbers, the first-best and second-best, and maybe the third-best number as well in a very aggressive approach.

Following are the hottest numbers:

THREE-BALL LOTTERY HOTTEST NUMBERS					
1st Pos	**Freq**	**2nd Pos**	**Freq**	**3rd Pos**	**Freq**
7	19	0	16	2	15
6	17	3	15	4	15
0	16	9	15	8	15
4	11	8	14	3	14
9	10	1	11	1	10

Money management is always a concern when wagering—and lottery and lotto are as much gambling games as are sports betting and casino games—though of course you want good coverage of your very best numbers. Picking the top one, two or three numbers gives you just that—and again, you don't have to play all three best numbers in all columns. You want to keep your budget for lottery tickets to a manageable amount.

These are the numbers you have chosen:

YOUR CHOSEN NUMBERS		
Position 1	**Position 2**	**Position 3**
7	0	2
	3	4
	9	8

In Position 1, the 7, 6 and 0-balls are obvious candidates due to their strength in performance, and in the next two positions, the 0 and 2 respectively are obvious choices as they are the best-performing numbers. But you're going to play aggressively and add the ties in the second and third positions as well. Why not the 0 ball in the first position? It has performed better than all the other numbers except the 0 ball in the second position, where it is tied in frequency of occurrence.

And if not the 0, why not the 6 in the first position? It's an even better-performing number than the 0!

Clearly, you could have chosen these numbers, but you have to draw the line somewhere in the number of tickets you play. There is also another reason: Why is the 7 the only number chosen in the first position to the exclusion of two other high-performing numbers?

There is a plan and you'll see that in just a few seconds! Let's put some punch in the program and step it up a level.

ADDING KEYS TO YOUR PLAYS

What are we up to? You're going to play a master key, a number that gets played on all tickets!

The obvious choice for a master key is the 7 in the first position. Outperforming all other numbers, the number 7 is so strong that you want to play it on *all* your tickets. That is why we shunned the other two strong numbers in the first position. When a master key number is designated, there cannot be any other numbers chosen in the same position since the master key must be on every ticket.

Also, when just one number appears in a position, it is by default a master key because at least one number must be played in every position. There are no other numbers in the position from which to form a ticket!

Of course, you could hedge your bets and add the 6 and 0 balls, but in this case you decided not to because you want to limit the number of tickets you're buying to just six. You don't want to spend the money needed to cover every combination—that would be way over your budget—and you're banking on your best number to lead the way. If you extend your ticket coverage to 10 or 15 tickets, you could expand your number zone and play a second number in the first position (obviously, you downgrade the master to a major or minor) or you could get fuller coverage overall, still leaning on the master 7 in the first position.

If you wish to choose more than one number in a position—for example, adding the 6-ball to the first position—you must remove the master key designation for the 7 and work instead with one of the other three types of keys (major, minor and third key). But doing this with a budget of just six tickets doesn't give you a lot room to play with. You just don't have enough tickets to play too many numbers, particularly multiple keys.

You could look at playing the three strong numbers in the first position and just the top performers in the other two positions with a lineup such as this:

YOUR CHOSEN NUMBERS		
Position 1	**Position 2**	**Position 3**
7	0	2
6		
5		

The issue here, however, is that you're now playing the second and third position as masters! The 0 and 2 in the second and third position respectively would, by default as the only possibilities, be on every ticket! This would not be your intention, but there are no other chosen numbers in the pool. The 0 and 2 in the second and third position are not your strongest performing numbers. It's ironic that focusing on your three top numbers in the first position ends up shifting the balance of strength to the other positions.

That is why you concentrate your focus on promoting the best-performing numbers into keys and not let a default situation sway your focus away from your strength.

YOUR WHEELED NUMBERS

Here again are the chosen numbers from the last chart. The 7 in the first position is in bold type to indicate that you are playing it as a key. Since it is the only number in its column, the 7 acts as a master key to be played on all tickets because it is your top-performing number.

YOUR CHOSEN NUMBERS

Position 1	Position 2	Position 3
7	0	2
	3	4
	9	8

Note: Where a master key is designated, there cannot be any other numbers chosen in the same position since the master key will be on every ticket. Numbers cannot be duplicated in wheels so where a master is designated, meaning it will appear on all tickets, it replaces the selected number in the same position. If the key is a major, minor or third key, you can have multiple numbers in a position.

If you didn't play the 8 in last position, you could cover every number in a full wheel and your tickets would look like this:

7-0-2
7-0-4
7-3-2
7-3-4
7-9-2
7-9-4

But you do want to play the 8. Playing a full wheel is over your budget, so you assemble a regular wheel, which could look like this:

7-0-2
7-0-4
7-3-2
7-3-8
7-9-4
7-9-8

You can re-form the wheel with new parameters by adjusting the variables, as we discussed above. If you wanted to play all variables, three more tickets would have to be played and the complete set of tickets in a full wheel would be as follows:

7-0-2
7-0-4
7-0-8
7-3-2
7-3-4
7-3-8
7-9-2
7-9-4
7-9-8

In this case you could play all your tickets for a cost of $9. If you add more chosen numbers to a three-ball game, the cost of a full wheel goes up each time the possibilities expand.

LEVEL III LOTTERY: OTHER WINNING ANALYSES

I have shown a Best Number Analysis in the examples and a 100-game regression, but there are many other ways to attack three-ball and four-ball lottery games.

You could run different levels of regression such as 50, 150 or 250 games, or use other types of core analysis such as an Overdue Number Analysis, to choose your numbers. You could also apply Level II keys such as kings, queens, dukes, earls, lucky numbers and courts as I've shown earlier, or run exotic Level III strategies.

MORE ON FOUR-BALL STRATEGY

Everything you do in a three-ball analysis applies equally to the four-ball game except, of course, there is one extra ball drawn. But the approach to one game—with the exception of selecting numbers for that one extra ball—is identical to the other one. The process, the analysis, the strategies, and the thinking work exactly the same way.

The extra ball in four-ball lottery compared to three-ball lottery games accounts for *ten times* as many combinations as the three-ball drawing. What a difference one extra ball will make! The possibilities extend from 0-0-0-0 to 9-9-9-9 for a total of 10,000 possible number combinations. Compare that to the 1,000 combinations of the three-ball lottery.

As with the three-ball lotteries, you will track by digits and record the results in columns. Either that or wait almost *three decades* of daily drawings for each combination to be drawn exactly once before a repeated combination occurs —actually, a bit over 27 years. Technically, since many numbers would repeat before others occurred a single time, it would likely be considerably longer than 27 years. Anyway, you get the point: It is not practical to track combinations in three-ball lottery and incredibly less practical in the four-ball version.

With the addition of an extra position in a four-ball game, so many more tickets are possible that covering all our chosen numbers in a full wheel would get expensive. In these cases, an efficient wheel becomes that much more valuable—and necessary.

As in the three-ball game, positional analysis in four-ball lottery allows you to run different types of analyses to identify trends, streaks, tendencies, best numbers, overdue balls, clusters, combinations and a host of other data that you can extract to form your winning tickets. Under the theory that there is a bias or tendency in numbers drawn, you extract data from the positional analysis to identify the top-performing numbers and patterns in each position, which allows your advanced wheeling systems to create an optimal package of tickets. You can add key and lucky numbers, and make exotic plays using king, queen, duke, earl, court, wizard and other exotic keys for your tickets.

Once you have chosen the top numbers in each of the positions—just like the three-ball game—you run a wheeling system to optimize and form your best package of tickets.

And wait, hopefully, for the balls that will set you free!

12

FIVE-BALL & SIX-BALL LEVEL III LOTTO STRATEGIES

The five-ball and six-ball lotto games are incredibly popular in many jurisdictions and are regularly played by millions and millions of players.

One reason they are popular: Millionaires are made all the time. One version of six-ball lotto is the 6/49 game. The first number before the slash mark indicates the number of winning numbers you need and the second shows the total number of balls in the pool. As I talked about earlier, there are a panoply of versions, including 6/51, which has a pool of 51 numbers from which the six winning balls will be drawn, 6/54, which has a pool of 54 numbers, and lotto games with fewer total balls in the pool such as 6/42, 6/46 and 6/47.

THE EFFECT OF MORE BALLS IN THE POOL

What significance does the larger second number have for you? Quite a lot actually. Each extra ball in the pool makes it progressively more difficult to hit the jackpot.

Of course, every other player faces the same obstacles, but you would rather have it easier than harder to win a jackpot.

Your chances of winning a jackpot is your concern, not the uphill battles faced by other players.

Well, that's one way to look at it. There is another side of the coin! The harder it is to hit a jackpot, the greater in size that jackpot tends to grow. And as we all know, when a jackpot gets really big, excitement grows. In the old days, a $1 million jackpot would stir up people's blood. But that was then. Today you need jackpots in the hundreds of millions to raise blood pressure.

And when jackpots get that big, it seems everybody gets a little more flush in color when they think about the possibilities.

In any case, whether you prefer a smaller jackpot that is easier to hit—but never "easy" no matter what state game you play—or one that climbs to monstrous proportions, you'll often be limited to the game that is geographically convenient for you to play. Or when you are near a state border and have a ready choice, you can decide which game excites you or at least is a more attractive offering for your tastes.

If you do have a choice, one philosophy says that you're better off with a 6/49 game than a 6/54 game because, while the odds are ridiculously long in 6/49, they at least are not much more ridiculously long than in 6/54. (See, I didn't throw any big numbers at you so you can give me a pass on that questionable stretch of English.)

Another philosophical viewpoint says that if you want to go big, go really big. That's why you're playing the lotto in the first place. Again, when you have a choice, you decide which lotto game is the right one for you.

In any case, since the 6/49 is a common lotto game, we'll use that game in our strategy examples. But note that the exact same strategy shown below applies to every five-ball and six-ball lotto game, regardless of the number of balls in the pool. Let's get to the winning strategies now.

FREQUENCY ANALYSIS

All the lotto strategies you will use rely on gathering a history of prior draws so that you can extract information that you will use to choose the best numbers to play. You need to know the numbers that have distinguished themselves and have created a pattern worthy of your attention — and money.

That is where a frequency analysis comes in, the foundation of our approach to beating the lotto. Like the ancient saying "All roads lead to Rome," all roads in lotto emanate from a frequency analysis. This is the best way to identify the patterns and texture of the prior drawings from which you will formulate your strategies.

Of course, the easiest way to run a frequency analysis is to let an online strategy program do the work for you. For example, lotterysupersystem.com will perform the core analysis you need for just about any lotto game you come across. This is by far the best and easiest way to extract the desired results.

But let's say that you don't have a computer or are reluctant to use it, or you simply want to compile results by hand to get a careful forensic look at the inner workings of previous drawings before you put together a winning group of tickets. I've got you covered.

This is how you would do it:

11 STEPS TO MAKING A WINNING GROUP OF LOTTO TICKETS

1. CHOOSE YOUR GAME

You typically have various games from which to choose, from instant games to a few state-run games to multi-state games. You live in Dallas and like the Texas Lotto 6/54 offering, so you set your sights on winning that game.

Action: You play the Texas 6/54 game.

2. DECIDE REGRESSION LEVEL (LENGTH OF GAME HISTORY)

Once you have chosen the five-ball or six-ball lotto game you will be playing (or multi-state game that has a five-ball component), you have to decide how many recent games you want to track. There are various philosophies on the number of games that are ideal to track, and certain strategies specify an exact number of games, but for now, you'll use a regression level of 150 games. In chapter 7, *Level I Play: Core Strategies*, you learned how to do this.

Action: You run a Raw Frequency Analysis with a regression level of 150 games and display the raw data in chart form.

3. CONVERT RAW DATA INTO A MORE USABLE FORM

It's more difficult to draw conclusions from a sheet of dots, so you convert the raw data into a more usable form and create a Refined Frequency Analysis Chart.

Action: You convert raw data into numbers for ease of use.

4. SORT DATA

You sort the data from the previous chart by most-frequently drawn number over the specified number of drawings to least-frequently drawn number. In other words, you create a Best Number Frequency Analysis Chart. (See following page.)

Action: Sort data.

5. DETERMINE LEVEL I CORE STRATEGY & ANALYZE DATA

Now that you have the sorted data to work with, you see a good picture of the previous 100 drawings and have a lot of information to work with.

So what are you going to do with this information?

Aha! Now here is where you determine the approach you want to take in the 6/49 lotto game, or whatever lotto game you may be playing. You have various core strategies to choose from, the most basic structures being a Best Number Analysis (charting hot numbers) and an overdue number analysis (charting cold numbers). You could also work with a cluster analysis or an exotic. You decide to stick with the most popular core strategy, the very straightforward best number strategy.

Action: Determine Level I core strategy.

BEST NUMBER FREQUENCY ANALYSIS
150 Games / 6/54 Lotto Game

Best Number	Frequency	Rank
21	27	1
4	25	2
34	23	3
8	22	4
27	21	5
29	21	6
6	20	7
12	20	8
31	20	9
38	20	10
42	20	11
49	20	12
14	19	13
26	19	14
54	19	15
7	18	16
9	18	17
35	18	18
37	18	19
43	18	20
44	18	21
45	18	22
52	18	23
2	17	24
3	17	25

6. CHOOSE YOUR COVERAGE POOL OF CHOSEN NUMBERS

How many numbers do you want in your chosen number pool? Now is the time to decide. You have the sorted data in front of you. If you feel strongly about your pool, you can expand the coverage and if you feel less strongly, you can constrict the coverage.

You peruse your results carefully, going back and forth between a pool of 11 numbers and 10 numbers, and ultimately decide that 10 numbers should be part of your pool. You want the heavier number coverage afforded by fewer numbers.

Action: You decide on 10 chosen numbers for your pool.

7. GO TO LEVEL II: ADD KEY NUMBERS

It is perfectly fine to stick to the powerful Level I core strategies and avoid the more difficult Level II plays. But if you want to take your game up a notch, you'll want to work with key numbers. You have the option of working with kings, queen, earls, dukes, wizards and many of the other advanced plays available, including lucky numbers, all of which was covered in Chapter 8, *Level II Strategies: Key Numbers*.

You have a decision here and as you learn more and get comfortable with the core strategies and key numbers, you'll find your comfort zone.

If you decide to play only Level I strategies, skip ahead to step 8 (bypassing step 7).

Action: Take it to Level II and add key numbers.

8. DETERMINE THE NUMBER OF TICKETS YOU WANT TO PLAY

Okay, you have determined your strategy and have generated the numbers you want to work with. Now how do you work with them? Without straying into the territory of money management, which is an essential and very important separate topic carefully addressed later on, you need to choose the number of tickets you want to play. Five tickets? 10 tickets? 20 tickets? Less? More?

The number of tickets you want to play is really a question of how much money you're comfortable betting and what amount you can afford to lose without stretching yourself too thin or being foolish and reckless. Let's say you decide to play six tickets. You've already formed a pool of 10 chosen numbers, all of which give you a high enough confidence to play them.

How do you combine them to their greatest effectiveness? With a wheel, of course. But let's organize ourselves first.

Action: You decide to play six tickets.

9. CREATE A STRATEGY PROFILE

I like to get my numbers and strategy organized in a formal manner before making tickets, and the best way to do that is to create a strategy profile. A strategy profile displays the basic information you will be working with in putting your tickets together—the game being played, strategy used, regression level, number of tickets being bought, and the total pool of numbers, including chosen numbers and keys.

It would look like this:

STRATEGY PROFILE

Game	6-Ball Lotto (6/54)
Strategy	Best Number Analysis
Regression Level	150 Games
Number of Tickets	6
Total Pool of Numbers	10
Chosen Numbers	8
34, 8, 27, 29, 6, 12, 31, 38	
Keys	2
21	Master
4	Minor

Action: Create your strategy profile.

10. WHEEL YOUR NUMBERS

You choose a wheel that best matches the profile of numbers you'll play and either plug them in by hand (you can use Prof Jones' wheeling packages in the back of this book), or go online to LotterySuperSystem.com. The online software includes a range of wheels to best package your numbers into the tickets you want to play for maximum efficiency.

If your wheel features the hottest numbers over a specified amount of games, a fairly equal distribution of those chosen numbers will comprise your winning tickets if you have no keys. But we're playing keys here, so a higher confidence will be given to those numbers and they will appear in more tickets than the other chosen numbers.

These are the tickets the wheel created for you given the input you have provided. To rerun the wheel with new parameters, you would adjust the strategy profile.

Since there are a total of 10 chosen numbers (two of them keys), you use 10 letters, A through J.

LETTER CONVERSION CHART

A	B	C	D	E	F	G	H	I	J
21	4	34	8	27	29	6	12	31	38

WHEEL TEMPLATE
10 Chosen Numbers / 6 Tickets / 2 Keys

1.	A	B	C	D	E	F
2.	A	B	C	D	E	G
3.	A	B	E	H	I	J
4.	A	B	D	G	H	J
5.	A	B	F	H	I	J
6.	A	C	F	G	I	J

You replace the letters with the numbers from the letter conversion chart to form the tickets you'll play.

LEVEL II WHEEL
10 Chosen Numbers / 6 Tickets / 2 Keys

1.	21	4	34	8	27	29
2.	21	4	34	8	27	6
3.	21	4	27	12	31	38
4.	21	4	8	6	12	38
5.	21	4	29	12	31	38
6.	21	34	29	6	31	38

Each line going left to right represents a ticket of six numbers. There are six such lines, meaning you are betting six tickets.

The wheel has distributed the numbers, giving priority to the two most important numbers, your keys. The king, the 37, is a master key and is represented on all six tickets, while the 24, the queen, is played as a major key and appears on five of the six tickets. The other eight numbers are represented on three tickets each, except for the 41, which appears on four tickets. The keys are represented in bold type for easy identification. Note that the order in which the numbers are displayed is just to emphasize the keys, which is why they appear first in the tickets.

If there were no keys and your chart only contained chosen numbers, the wheel might distribute your numbers as follows:

WHEEL TEMPLATE
10 Chosen Numbers / 6 Tickets / 0 Keys

1.	A	B	C	D	E	H
2.	A	B	C	E	F	H
3.	A	B	D	G	I	J
4.	A	C	D	F	I	J
5.	B	E	F	G	H	J
6.	C	F	G	H	I	J

LEVEL I TEMPLATE
10 Chosen Numbers / 6 Tickets / 0 Keys

1.	21	4	34	8	27	12
2.	21	4	34	27	29	12
3.	21	4	8	6	31	38
4.	21	34	8	29	31	38
5.	4	27	29	6	12	38
6.	34	24	6	12	31	38

In this more evenly distributed wheel where no keys are in play, the ten chosen numbers you have selected to play appear either three or four times across the group of six tickets.

Appearing four times are the 3, 9, 15, 24, 37, 41 and appearing three times are the 18, 22, 26, and 38.

Action: Wheel your numbers.

11. BUY YOUR TICKETS

Okay, you've done all the work—you've chosen your game, decided on the length of game history, charted the raw results of the draws, converted the raw data into a more usable form, sorted your data, determined your strategy, selected your chosen numbers, added keys, determined the number of tickets you want to play, created a strategy profile, and wheeled your numbers.

Now it's time to go get your tickets and see how luck shines on you.

Action: Buy tickets and win!

THE 11 STEPS OF PUTTING TOGETHER A WINNING GROUP OF TICKETS

1. Choose Your Game
2. Decide Length of Game History
3. Convert Raw Data Into a More Usable Form
4. Sort Data
5. Determine Level I Core Strategy & Analyze Data
6. Choose Your Coverage of Chosen Numbers
7. Go to Level II: Add Key Numbers If Any
8. Determine the Number of Tickets You Want to Play
9. Create a Strategy Profile
10. Wheel Your Numbers
11. Buy Your Tickets

13

DUAL-POOL LEVEL III LOTTERY GAME STRATEGY

A number of multi-state lottery games feature massive multi-million dollar prizes that get players drooling for the astronomically large prizes that periodically increase to nosebleed amounts. As the windfall grows into the high tens of millions and then hundreds of millions, regular players and even casual non-players begin buying tickets like they're the last buckets of water in the desert, hoping to be the lucky individual that scores the headline-grabbing, life-changing draw.

The big multi-state games— Powerball, Mega Millions, Hot Lotto, Lucky for Life, Wild Card 2, 2by2, MegaHits and Tri-State Megabucks Plus—feature two pools of numbers, one set from which five balls are drawn, and a second set from which one ball is drawn. The games vary in the number of balls in the five-ball and one-ball pools.

These two-pool games are called **dual-pool games**.

THE WINNING APPROACH

You approach multi-state dual-pool games with the same approach as other lottery and lotto games, first analyzing the five-ball pool of numbers and then the single-ball pool to identify the top-performing balls to play. You analyze each pool separately to determine the chosen numbers and keys you will use as the foundation of your tickets.

Note that the strategies and analysis for one multi-state game will work for all multi-state games where winning balls are drawn from two or more pools of numbers. It doesn't matter whether the game is a multi-jurisdictional one or one operated by an individual government entity—the principles and strategies are the same.

We'll use Powerball as an example of how to create winning strategies for the huge multi-state games. First, let's review how these games work.

HOW TO PLAY DUAL-POOL GAMES

Powerball is one of the most popular dual-pool games. Like the 6/49 lotto games, six balls are drawn in Powerball, but unlike the standard 6/49 games, two separate bins are used for the draws. Five of those balls are drawn from a drum of 69 white balls and one ball is drawn from a separate drum of 26 red balls. Note that these relatively recent changes, enacted in October 2015, were made to increase interest in the game. Sales had been lagging, so the operators made the five-ball pool harder to hit, which meant the jackpots would grow much larger and more exciting. They did this by increasing the balls in the white pool from 59 to 69, and decreasing the balls in the red pool from 39 to 26.

The single red ball drawn is called the **Powerball**. To win a big jackpot as well as many of the larger prizes you must correctly pick the Powerball in addition to at least four correct white balls. You can also win a big prize without the Powerball, but you would have to correctly guess all five white balls drawn. Of course, what you really want to do is pick all five white balls and the red Powerball. That wins you the jackpot!

Mega Millions is another massive dual-pool game played in more than 40 states. There are also two pools, but the main pool in Mega Millions contains 75 white balls, numbered 1-75. The second pool, like Powerball, has only one ball, a gold colored one. This pool contains 15 balls, numbered 1-15. A few jackpots in Mega Millions have exceeded one-half billion dollars.

Unlike lottery games where order of draw is important, the order of draw in the five-ball pool of the multi-state games is irrelevant. If you pick all the numbers correctly, you win. It's as simple as that.

The drawn numbers are typically displayed in ascending order. They may also be published horizontally—like this: 3, 11, 19, 47, 52—or in chart form as follows:

POWERBALL
Display of Five Drawn White Balls
3
11
19
47
52

In either case, those would be the winning balls.

MULTI-STATE PAYOUTS

Each game has its own prize payment structure that is published and readily available to players. Note that in California, which is an exception to the prize pools offered in other states for the big games, all prizes in the dual-pool games are pari-mutuel, meaning that the payouts are based on sales, like standard lotto games—that is, the more tickets sold, the larger the prizes.

Following are the standard prize pools for the two largest dual-pool games, Powerball and Mega Millions:

POWERBALL PAYOUTS

BASIC POWERBALL	PAYOUTS
5 White Balls and the Powerball	Jackpot!
5 White Balls, no Powerball	$100,0000
4 White Balls and the Powerball	$50,000
4 White Balls, no Powerball	$100
3 White Balls and the Powerball	$100
3 White Balls, no Powerball	$7
2 White Balls and the Powerball	$7
1 White Ball and the Powerball	$4
Only the Powerball	$4

Power Play is an extra bet you can make for $1—it must be purchased at the same time as the Powerball ticket—that allows you to increase your potential prize amounts (except for the jackpot) by a multiple of 2x, 3x, 4x, 5x or 10x.

MEGA MILLIONS PAYOUTS

BASIC MEGA MILLIONS	PAYOUTS
5 White Balls and the Gold Ball	Jackpot!
5 White Balls, no Gold Ball	$1,000,000
4 White Balls and the Gold Ball	$5,000
4 White Balls, no Gold Ball	$500
3 White Balls and the Gold Ball	$50
3 White Balls, no Gold Ball	$5
2 White Balls and the Gold Ball	$5
1 White Ball and the Gold Ball	$2
Only the Gold Ball	$1

Note that any set prizes or **Megaplier** prizes, including the Match 5+0 prize, may be reduced if wins exceed the available prize fund.

Mega Millions also offers a multiplier option that gives you, for $1 more, the chance to multiply your winning prizes—with the exception of the jackpot—by 2x, 3x, 4x and 5x.

MULTI-STATE DUAL-POOL ANALYSIS

Powerball and the other dual-pool games featuring prize pools that reach into the hundreds of millions of dollars and garner national attention as the jackpot grows larger and larger are actually two games in one—a five-ball lotto game along with a one-ball lottery game all rolled into one contest.

In these multi-state games that feature balls drawn from two separate drums, you analyze each pool separately to determine the best balls to play. You rely on a frequency analysis to grab results from the five-ball pool—the same method you use for five-ball and six-ball lotto games. You have to decide which of the many strategy analyses—such as best number, overdue and cluster—you'll use to isolate your chosen numbers, and how long a history would be optimal for the situation.

You might run it solid and grab a history of 100 games, or run it long with a regression level of 150 or even 250 games for your results. You might decide instead to go with a burst strategy, taking a very recent history of, say, 10 games or so.

The second pool with one ball gets analyzed separately as if it were a lottery drawing. Since only one ball is being tracked, a simple one-column Positional Analysis would suffice. It might look like this if you were playing Mega Millions (15-ball pool of gold balls) and ran a regression level of 50 games.

POSITIONAL ANALYSIS RAW CHART
1-Ball Mega Millions / 50 Drawings

	1-Ball
1	•••••
2	••
3	••••
4	•••••••••
5	••
6	••••
7	•••
8	
9	•••••
10	•••••••
11	
12	••
13	•••
14	••
15	••••

You analyze the Positional Analysis Raw Chart to isolate the top-performing numbers for your analyses and place those numbers into your pool of chosen numbers.

WORKING WITH KEYS

The dual-pool games present an interesting challenge for advanced players. You want to keep your ticket purchases to a reasonable amount, but at the same time, each pool presents you with situations where you might want to elevate chosen numbers to keys. There are a lot of numbers to work with and two pools, which is why these games are so tough to beat—and so tempting to chase with an aggressive group of tickets.

Let's start with the larger pool of 69 numbers. You may find one ball or several balls that greatly outperform the others and are deserving of key status. In the other pool, you may also find one or more numbers that you want to promote to keys as well. You'll have to balance the keys in the dual pools to maximize your coverage, while also trying to keep your ticket cost to a reasonable amount. There could even be situations where you use two strong one-ball keys out of the one-ball pool and create separate pools of betting with them.

You can see why wheels are so important in two-pool games. You need a way to get a reasonable net of coverage while putting your chosen numbers and keys in play at a modest cost. For example, you could run two separate keys with the same pool of chosen numbers. Let's look at that.

ROTATING MASTER KEY

Let's start with a strategy profile you would use for a dual-pool game.

STRATEGY PROFILE

Game	Powerball
Strategy	Best Number Analysis
Regression Level	100 Games
Number of Tickets	12
White Pool	5-Ball Pool
Total Pool of Numbers	9
Chosen Numbers	9
11, 14, 18, 19, 23, 25, 36, 39, 40	
Keys	0
Red Pool	1-Ball Pool
Total Pool of Numbers	2
Chosen Numbers	0
Keys	2
5, 21	

LETTER CONVERSION CHART

<u>A</u>	<u>B</u>	<u>C</u>	<u>D</u>	<u>E</u>	<u>F</u>	<u>G</u>	<u>H</u>	<u>I</u>	<u>J</u>	<u>K</u>
5	21	11	14	18	19	23	25	36	39	40

WHEEL TEMPLATE
11 Chosen Numbers / 6 Tickets / Split Rotating Key

1.	A	C	E	F	G	I
2.	A	C	E	F	H	J
3.	A	C	D	F	H	J
4.	A	D	E	F	I	K
5.	A	D	G	H	I	K
6.	A	C	G	I	J	K

WHEEL TEMPLATE
11 Chosen Numbers / 6 Tickets / Split Rotating Key

1.	B	C	E	F	G	I
2.	B	C	E	F	H	J
3.	B	C	D	F	H	J
4.	B	D	E	F	I	K
5.	B	D	G	H	I	K
6.	B	C	G	I	J	K

Your wheels created these 12 tickets:

FIRST ROTATING MASTER KEY GROUP

1-ball	5-ball pool
5	11, 18, 19, 23, 36
5	11, 18, 19, 25, 39
5	11, 14, 19, 25, 39
5	14, 18, 19, 36, 40
5	14, 23, 25, 36, 40
5	11, 23, 36, 39, 40

SECOND ROTATING MASTER KEY GROUP

1-ball	5-ball pool
21	11, 18, 19, 23, 36
21	11, 18, 19, 25, 39
21	11, 14, 19, 25, 39
21	14, 18, 19, 36, 40
21	14, 23, 25, 36, 40
21	11, 23, 36, 39, 40

In this second pool, the only number that was changed was the 1-ball number, using the 21 as a master key instead of the 5. This type of rotation, where a master key in one group (either the 1-ball group or the 5-ball group) is replaced by a different master key, is called a **rotating master key**. The rest of the numbers in the tickets are identical in the first and second groups. You use a rotating master key when you feel so strongly about the strength of two masters that you use them separately with an identical group of chosen numbers so as not to dilute the play.

DUAL MASTER KEY

Let's say you wanted to use the 11 as an additional major key for the 5-ball pool in the second group. We'll use the following wheel template:

WHEEL TEMPLATE					
11 Chosen Numbers / 6 Tickets / Split Key					
1. B	C	D	E	G	I
2. B	C	D	F	H	J
3. B	C	D	F	H	J
4. B	C	E	F	I	K
5. B	C	G	H	I	K
6. B	C	E	G	J	K

Your ticket might look like this:

SECOND MASTER KEY GROUP WITH 5-BALL KEY

1-ball	5-ball pool
21	11, 14, 18, 23, 36
21	11, 14, 19, 25, 39
21	11, 14, 19, 25, 39
21	11, 18, 19, 36, 40
21	11, 23, 25, 36, 40
21	11, 18, 23, 39, 40

In this group, the 11 is played as a master key in the five-ball pool, and the rest of the numbers are given equal distribution appearing on three tickets each. If you were playing just six tickets, this particular group would have two master keys in play since the 21 is being used as a master in the one-ball group. This is called a **dual master key**. (Note: You can only have dual master keys in dual-pool games.)

SECTION V

THE COMPLETE LOTTERY PLAYER

14

THE FINANCIAL PLAN

It costs money to play lottery and lotto games but you buy tickets because you want a shot at breaking free in life with a huge win. And the more tickets you buy, the more chances you have of winning. In this chapter we're going to talk about the financial implications of playing the lottery games—money management, the most important element of any gambling game—including how much you should invest and what happens if you win.

These are essential discussions, but the most critical is the all-important, all-encompassing concept of money management.

We'll start with that.

MONEY MANAGEMENT

The more tickets you play the greater your chances of winning prizes. That goes for all lottery and lotto games regardless of format, as well as bingo, raffles, keno and any other type of game where a drawing is involved. There are many lotto and lottery games out there—three-ball, four-ball, five-ball, six-ball, Powerball and many other variations, you name it. And they all share that same principle: Play more tickets, increase your chances to win more prizes.

But that comes at a cost. More money. Everyone can figure that out. But what everyone does not figure out is exactly the cost of that cost. At least, not until it's too late. There are numerous stories of people who have slowly or rapidly invested their life savings in the games by following "the more, the better" theory.

You can make a lot of money playing lottery and lotto games — after all, that's why you chase jackpots every week and why you purchased this book — but at the same time, an aggressive player can get drained of needed resources if he consistently chases too hard week in and week out. As in all forms of gambling, it is important to view lottery games as a form of entertainment and to allocate a budget for that entertainment.

In other words, you must gamble within your means.

You have to decide how much money you have available as an entertainment budget. There is no guarantee of winning in any form of gambling, no matter how perfectly the stars may align, and that is certainly the case when playing the lottery. You'll have small wins along the way and weeks where you don't cash a single ticket. You can't ever expect to win money, that's just not practical. Overall, you're playing against big odds at the lottery and those odds are very hard to overcome. It is prudent to remind you that there are only a relatively few big jackpot winners, and you might not become one of those few. Meanwhile, week in and week out — if you are a weekly player — the lottery games will steadily ding your funds.

You must be able to handle the losses. Conversely, if you win, you have to be able to handle the wins.

Players are enticed by the big jackpots that can be won with the purchase of a single $1 ticket or a group of such tickets.

Where else in life can you hope to get such massive payouts for such a small investment? When the jackpots get bigger and bigger and hit hundreds of millions of dollars, lottery fever goes wild and the net of players increases, making the jackpots larger and the frenzy even greater.

And everyone is thinking, "That just might be me." You know something? Yes, it just might be. *You might be the next $100 million winner!*

Let's go back to that $1 ticket. It's not much of an investment for the hope of hitting a life-changing jackpot. But the reality is that it's not just $1. The investment may be for five tickets for $5, or 10 tickets for $10. There are players who play an even greater number of tickets, betting $20, $25, $50 and even hundreds of dollars. That's *just for one week*. And there are lots of weeks in a year. Fifty-two of them, to be precise. You play the lotto weekly, or even daily, and that money adds up fast. For too many players, the lottery becomes a serious financial investment with not enough return.

So it's not just $1.

If you spend $20 per week on various tickets, your lottery investment will be over $1,000 in a year. For people scraping to get by, that might not be money well spent. One thousand dollars is not a trivial amount. Bigger players invest much more than that in the lottery. Much, much more. Do the real math of how much you spend yearly on lottery and lotto games and the cold, hard numbers might be scary.

So how much should you invest in the pursuit of the dream jackpot? What does your strategy suggest for an investment?

Both questions have a real easy answer. It's the same type of answer that all gamblers face—poker players, blackjack players, slots players, bingo players, whoever—but the answer is different for different people. It is this: Spend whatever amount makes sense for you and your life. Whatever your situation, you must always follow this dictate.

Never gamble with money you cannot afford to lose, either financially or emotionally.

You need to be smart with your money. If $20 a week cuts into your needs, you shouldn't be buying $20 worth of lottery tickets and certainly shouldn't be buying $30 or even $50 per week either. And if losing that $20 causes you to be emotionally upset, you have to ask yourself, "What am I doing?"

Be smart with your money, be smart with yourself. No gambling pursuit, no matter how favorable or attractive, guarantees that you will win. No matter how lucky you feel, it won't change the odds of a game and it won't change your chances of winning. You must be prepared to lose your investment, because it very well might happen. You should only play lottery and lotto games with discretionary income, money you don't mind losing and won't hurt you financially or emotionally if you do lose.

Sure, it's nice to pursue the dream, but not at the expense of reality. If you heed common sense and play within your emotional and financial needs, you'll never get hurt at the game.

And you know what? You just may get lucky.

WHAT A FOOL BELIEVES

There are some crazies who play lottery games—for example, the player who risks it all on one big play, dumping his entire playing bankroll into tickets hoping to strike it rich. He just needs to win that one drawing. Just that one drawing. Everything is aligned—the win is in his dreams, lots of little lucky things are happening that haven't happened before, the timing is right. He just *feels* it. He's thinking he can't go wrong with all those winning omens? And he waits for the lucky day, the day that will change his life.

He waits with great anticipation and the day finally arrives. Everything, just everything, is perfect. He eagerly watches as the balls are announced.

First number, 17. Good! Got it right. He knew that number was the right one. It was his big number, the can't-miss one. Second number, 4. Score! Had that right too. What a great start. Dreams of grandeur permeate his mind. He pictures money piled so high he gets drunk off the smell of the ink. Third number, fourth number, fifth number, nothing. Depression falls like the winter night in Lapland. Too little, too late. Three correct picks wins a measly amount on some tickets, but the rest of the load gets stuck on those first two numbers and advance no further. Thousands of dollars are lost. It's a disaster. All his extra money has just been lost on one impulsive, idiotic play.

The gambler was right: It was a lucky day, but it was bad luck. All his savings are gone. "What a fool!" he thinks. And he is right. What a fool.

There is another version of this: the slow weekly grind of putting too much money on lottery tickets at the expense of needed savings, food, things for the kids, something Mom or Dad needs. Rent is tight. And every week, the drain of the lottery, only broken up here and there by smaller wins that serve as starter fuel for more lottery tickets and don't solve anything. Pretty soon that same thousand dollars or thousands of dollars gets lost, only more slowly than the fool lost it.

All wrong! And badly so. It's okay to dream, it's okay to take a shot at the dream. But taking it that far is a sad statement on life.

It's not the idiotic thinking behind these actions that is the sad part. Sure, more tickets give you more chances, but the odds are so deeply stacked against players that this pipe dream is really dangerous. No, the sad part is that almost every single time, these foolish people decimate their life savings. They're gambling, and they're gambling at a game with worse odds than any casino would offer them. They don't understand that this investment isn't really an investment, but a risky gamble, and even worse, a pipe dream.

If you're going to play lottery and lotto games, you have to be smart. That is why this chapter was written for you. It's easy to get carried away like an intoxicated fool and do things you normally wouldn't do, either in one idiotic maneuver or slowly over time, with actions that are greatly to your detriment.

You have to make sensible decisions with your lottery money. You must be able to afford losing the money you risk. You must enjoy wagering that money—only then does playing the lottery and chasing the dream make sense.

In any one drawing or number of drawings, anything can happen. You may run cold for a while—that's normal in any form of gambling and number selection no matter how well you've planned your bets—but keep your spirits up and stick to your program.

CASHING OUT A BIG JACKPOT

If you hit the big jackpot, you sometimes get the choice of taking the money all at once, or taking the payments spread out over 20 years.

How do you play it?

If you're strictly looking at getting the most money possible, generally speaking there is nothing to think about—you take the money in one lump sum. You have control of the money; you can collect interest on the money; you can do whatever you want.

But there are other considerations.

If you're a person who doesn't handle money well, or if you're prone to giving in to the pressures of friends, family and neighbors who sometimes charge in to grab a share of your winnings—ironically, far too many of these stories have been told by jackpot winners whose lives were ruined by winning the lottery—then you are far better off taking the 20- or 30-year annuity of winnings or however the payment works out. Every year, that big check is going to arrive and keep you on easy street.

There are many people—such as lottery winners, sports stars and actors—who have never had much money and then suddenly get a massive windfall. They don't know how to handle the tens and hundreds of millions of dollars that are suddenly dumped in their lap. It is an endless pool of money, that is, until it runs out. The hangers-on, the financial advisors, the lavish lifestyle, the outlandishly wasteful purchases, the loans, the business investments, and the greedy hands of others grab and grab until one day there is nothing left. And the former lottery millionaire wakes up to find himself flat broke.

Don't let that be you.

If you are prone to this money grab, just take your money in the installments. It's the safest way.

But if you manage your money well and are not prone to the pitfalls of monetary success, you are much better off taking the jackpot in one fell swoop if you can grab it. The value of the jackpot will generally be far superior to what you'd be getting by waiting out a lifetime of payouts, often with no interest.

WHAT IF YOU WIN THE BIG ONE?
A dream has come true. Or has it?

I met the first million-dollar lottery jackpot winner many years ago when we were both interviewed on the same TV show. He won the jackpot back when a million dollars was really a lot of money—but his tale was anything but happy. In fact, he said that winning the lottery was one of the worst things that had ever happened to him. And he's not the only one.

A similar thing occurs to many winners. Every close and near relative, every close and near friend crawl out of the woodwork feeling that they are entitled to your help because you're rich. Then the financial experts, as well as the hucksters and hustlers, track you down. If you get entangled with this nefarious group, you have another set of problems. Welcome to the world of the **lottery termite**, a leech that attempts to get his chance to eat up your lottery money.

At the end of the day, you may have won a million or millions, but you've also inherited—or at least they all want you to inherit—the lottery termite's problems and plans. "Can you help me with this little medical procedure I need?" "I need a little push to get out from under this credit card bill that has crept up on me." "I need this." "I need that." "Hey, you got a lot of money, can you loan me $50,000 for this great can't-miss business idea? I'll get it back to you in six months."

Uh-huh.

That first million-dollar winner I spoke about got ruined by a whole crop of these people. They made his life so miserable he wished he'd never won that "life-changing" prize. It changed his life all right, just not in the right way. People he barely knew or hadn't seen in years came crawling out of the woodwork imploring him to give them money. The lottery termites ate away at him. It originally seemed like he had lucked into heaven, but it became a living hell—until he had none of the lottery money left and could resume his life as he had lived it before.

Let's learn from this.

My advice is simple: You won the money, it's yours. Other people's problems are their problems. They are not your problems. Of course, you might help out immediate close family and friends, but beyond that you are not responsible for your second, third and seventeenth cousins and the other leaches and parasites that find their way to your door.

For what it's worth.

In any case, if you hit it big, enjoy it. Do what makes *you* happy, not what would make other people happy. Sometimes, those goals coincide, great. But when they don't, don't get sucked into someone else's cesspool.

Enjoy your jackpot. Vacation like crazy. Buy things you'd like. Put money away in a safe place so that you have a healthy cushion. Just figure out what would make you happy and use the money to help achieve that end. If this book helped you get there, let me know. Write to me at lotterysupersystem.com. Tips accepted.

And congratulations. You're rich!!!

15

THE ODDS OF WINNING

THE ODDS ARE THE ODDS

Let's not sugarcoat this. The odds against winning a big jackpot are astronomical, no matter what strategy you employ, and your chances of winning overall—between small wins, medium wins, and jackpots—are poor. Lottery and lotto are negative expectation games and the odds of coming out ahead are greatly against you. The state-run games or any other entity running a lottery or lotto type game have a huge mathematical edge over you and no amount of strategy and number prediction changes these expectations.

So why play the game?

People like chasing the big dream. When jackpots get huge, lottery and lotto players get excited. Casual players get in on the act making sure to get their tickets in so that they too will have a shot at the dream. People who never or rarely play the game get excited as well—hundreds of millions of dollars out there for grabs does that to people—and they too get in on the action. And the jackpot grows even bigger, along with the concomitant excitement, press coverage, and imaginations of millions of people thinking this jackpot just might be theirs for the taking.

But let me make this clear: If playing lottery games is your idea of making a living, it is a very bad idea. The odds are stacked high against you, so high in the sky you can't even see the top of the imaginary wall. What the exact odds are depends upon the game. But whatever the game may be, you can count on the odds being big-time against you and you can count on it costing you big in the long run—unless you are one of the lucky few that catch the dream. Lottery proceeds are large contributors to the economies of state governments, which use lottery games to finance all sorts of state programs.

Guess who all that money comes from? You're right—you and your fellow players.

People do win, of course, and that's why others play. They get inspired by stories of players who have struck it rich. As the slogan of the New York lottery goes, "Hey, you never know." But like all forms of gambling, you have to manage your money wisely. I won't belabor that point too much here—we covered that carefully in the money management section—I just want to advise you against blindly chasing the pie in the sky while ignoring the realities.

If you follow the strategies in this book, your chances of winning will increase. Be warned, however, that they do not change the fundamental percentage disadvantage you face in the lottery games you play. But like I said in *The Theory of Beating the Lottery* chapter, if you subscribe to the theory that past winning results affect future draws, as many players do, or are looking for a way to make the game more fun and give you a plan, the strategies in this book give you a fantastic approach for trying to beat lottery and lotto games.

JACKPOTS AND THE NUMBER OF BALLS IN THE POOL

If you observe lottery games long enough, you will see a big difference between the 49-ball games and ones with larger amounts of balls used in play—and lesser amounts too. Quite simply, the more balls in play, the harder it is for you to win. The monster jackpots that grab national attention tend to be those games with more balls, and therefore more obstacles toward winning. Each ball that gets added to a pool of 49 balls (the 6/49 game) greatly increases the difficulty of choosing all six balls correctly, which is why lotto games with 54 balls take longer for a winning combination to be reached than a 49-ball pool, and even longer for games like Mega Millions and Powerball.

Conversely, the jackpots in games drawing from a smaller pool than the 49 we're using as an example get hit more often than the 6/49 games.

In a 6/25 lotto game (six balls are picked from a pool of 25 total balls), your chances of choosing all six numbers with one ticket are 1 in 177,100. In a 6/49 game, picking all six balls correctly has odds of 1 in 13,983,816. If the game is a 6/54, your chances of choosing all six numbers correctly out of the 54 balls in the pool with one ticket balloons to 1 in 25,827,165. That's just one chance in more than twenty-five million, astronomically difficult odds. That's quite a difference between the various games. As I stated earlier, you went from astronomical odds of hitting the jackpot to much more astronomical odds.

ODDS OF HITTING THE BIG JACKPOT

Game	Odds
6/25	1 in 177,100
6/49	1 in 13, 983,816
6/54	1 in 25,827,165
Mega Millions	1 in 258,890,850
Powerball	1 in 292,201,338

You have to keep in mind that it is very difficult to win a jackpot with these odds against you regardless of the strategy you choose or how hard you appeal to the heavens above.

You do increase the odds by playing better and obtaining more tickets, but you are still up against a mountain of difficulty. But then again, I understand that you're not playing for the odds but for the chance of beating them, hoping that a few dollars invested will change everything in your life. You want a shot at hitting it big. Really big.

It happens to many players, and it could happen to you.

The key concept in all gambling, and all investments, and all endeavors in life, is risk versus reward. You're not going to risk all your money if the upside is just a 10% gain. That would be a moronic move for even the most compulsive of gamblers. You might consider risking all your money if the payoff were a five times multiple.

I'm not saying that would be wise, but you would certainly run the idea through your brain. You might even consider the idea for double the payoff, though going for that latter payoff, given the risks, would be idiotic.

You would consider putting up 10% of your money to gain 12% interest on a safe investment, and maybe another 10% of your money on a risky investment that may return 50% of your original amount. But that's not *all* your money

But if it costs you just a few bucks to make millions, even hundreds of millions of dollars? Well, that's lottery and lotto.

That's why you play the game.

ODDS OF WINNING: 6/49 GAME

The 6/49 game gives you the following chances of getting a winner with a single ticket:

6/49 LOTTO GAME ODDS	
Balls	**Odds of Picking Winning Combination**
6	1 in 13,983,816
5	1 in 54,201
4	1 in 1,032
3	1 in 57
Odds to win any prize	1 in 54

ODDS OF POWERBALL AND MEGA MILLIONS

POWERBALL ODDS			
Match White Ball		Match Red Ball	Chances of Hitting*
5	and	1	1 in 292,201,338
5	and	0	1 in 11,688,054
4	and	1	1 in 913,129
4	and	0	1 in 36,525
3	and	1	1 in 14,494
3	and	0	1 in 579
2	and	1	1 in 701
1	and	1	1 in 92
0	and	1	1 in 38
Odds to win any prize			1 in 25

*Based on the standard $2 play. Numbers are rounded to nearest whole number.

POWER PLAY BET

Power Play is an extra $1 bet in Powerball that can be made—it must be purchased at the time you get your Powerball ticket—that allows you to increase your potential prize (except for the jackpot) by a multiple of 2x, 3x, 4x and 5x (or 10x when offered). In other words, if you choose a winning ticket that would normally pay $7 and you have purchased the Power Play option, you would win $35 if the multiplier were 5x.

Note that if a very popular number is drawn and there isn't enough money in the pool to cover it, your prize may be reduced.

POWER PLAY ODDS
With 10x Multiplier

Power Play	Odds
10x	1 in 43
5x	1 in 21.5
4x	1 in 14.33
3x	1 in 3.31
2x	1 in 1.70

POWER PLAY ODDS
No 10x Multiplier

Power Play	Odds
5x	1 in 21
4x	1 in 14
3x	1 in 3.23
2x	1 in 1.75

POWERPLAY ODDS

Match White Ball		Match Red Ball	Chances of Hitting*
5	and	1	1 in 292,201,338
5	and	0	1 in 11,688,054
4	and	1	1 in 913,129
4	and	0	1 in 36,525
3	and	1	1 in 14,494
3	and	0	1 in 579
2	and	1	1 in 701
1	and	1	1 in 92
0	and	1	1 in 38
Odds to win any prize			1 in 25

MEGA MILLIONS ODDS		
Match White Ball	**Match Gold Ball**	**Chances of Hitting**
5 and	1	1 in 258,890,850
5 and	0	1 in 18,492,204
4 and	1	1 in 739,688
4 and	0	1 in 52,835
3 and	1	1 in 10,720
3 and	0	1 in 766
2 and	1	1 in 473
1 and	1	1 in 56
0 and	1	1 in 21
Chance of hitting any prize		1 in 14.7

MEGAPLIER BET

Mega Millions also offers a multiplier option, called a **Megaplier**, which gives players, for $1 more, the chance to multiply their winning prizes by 2x, 3x, 4x, 5x, and sometimes 10x. Again, the exception is the jackpot. Winning a multiplier on a jackpot would be a losing proposition for Mega Millions (and Powerball as well), which is why they exclude the jackpot prize from the multiplier. As you know, they're in these games to make a killing, not to get killed. You're the prey, not them.

The Megaplier is a second drawing from a pool whose balls are numbered 2, 3, 4, and 5.

These are the odds of hitting the various multipliers:

MEGAPLIER ODDS	
Power Play	**Odds**
5x	1 in 2.5
4x	1 in 5
3x	1 in 3.75
2x	1 in 7.5

MULTIPLIER STRATEGY

Quite frankly, I don't like the multiplier bets (Powerplay, Megaplier and others of their ilk). In fact, I think they're stupid plays to make. We had a long discussion earlier about why you play lottery and lotto games and that was to hit it big. That's why you risk small amounts of money at ridiculously bad odds. For the dream.

So why double your potential winnings on scrap-heap money when your chances of winning are piss poor? It makes no sense.

If you want to gamble the extra money, play a wider net of tickets going for the big one. We talked about that earlier also. That greatly increases your chances of winning. Dump it in a casino where, at least, the poor bets are multiple times better than these yokel plays. Get an ice cream cone for yourself. Buy a knick-knack. Save a years' worth of these bets and get yourself something much nicer. Give a little bit to someone who is struggling and brighten his or her day.

Do anything but give those lousy multiplier bets to the greedy lottery operators.

THE REDS AND THE GREENS

There is a lot to gain by going after jackpots that have swelled to irresistibly giant sizes. Let me give you a simple example to show you how this mathematically benefits you.

There is a cup with 11 coins in it. Ten are green, and one is red. You make a bet on the red coin being drawn. The payout is eight coins for the red coin being drawn, giving the person booking the game a very healthy advantage over you. The true odds of winning are 10-1 against, but you are being paid only 8-1 on your wins—kind of like a carny-type casino game (think the Big Six wheel) or a game like keno.

Now the coin game runs a promotion and says they'll pay you nine coins if you choose the red coin. Your odds of winning haven't changed—they are still 10-1 against—however your benefit of winning has greatly improved because you are winning nine coins instead of eight coins. The "new" red-green gamble is still not a great game, but it is a much better game for you than earlier because of the bigger payout.

It's like the jackpot in a lottery game. When the prize pool goes way up, you still have the same bad odds, but the reward is so much greater that you are getting much more bang for your buck. In gambling terms, your payoff is much better.

7 WAYS TO INCREASE YOUR WINNING CHANCES OR PERCENTAGE OF RETURN

SHIFTING THINGS IN YOUR FAVOR

A $1 bet on a lottery ticket can win you millions, even hundreds of millions of dollars. Another way to look at this is that it takes millions of losing $1 tickets by other players to build a jackpot for you to win. There are ways to increase your odds or percentage of return, and we concentrate on these little gems of advice in this brief chapter.

Following is a list of the seven ways to either increase your odds of winning or your percentage of return:

7 WAYS TO INCREASE YOUR WINNING CHANCES OR PERCENTAGE OF RETURN

1. Use our strategies and wheels to make more winning tickets. If you normally play two tickets and use our Level II and Level III advanced plays and strategies to cover 10 tickets, your odds of winning have increased by 500%. The odds are still long, but you've greatly increased your shot at the big one (and the little ones too).

2. If frequency of wins is more important to you than going for a larger jackpot, play games with fewer balls in the pool. The fewer the number of balls in a lotto or dual-pool game, the greater your chances of winning. The more balls in the pool, the more difficult it is to hit the winning combination and, concomitantly, the larger the winning jackpots tend to be.

3. Play bigger jackpots. If all else is equal, you mathematically have a much bigger percentage return for your money on a huge jackpot game than one with simply a big jackpot. Lotto is a pari-mutuel game. The amount of money won is dependent on the amount of money bet. But forgetting how the money gets into the pool, go for games with bigger pools. Your odds of winning haven't changed, but the amount you can win compared to your bet has changed, making the game a better percentage play for you.

4. Avoid multiplier bets in games like Powerball and Mega Millions. Bad odds, little upside—don't bother.

5. When choosing lucky numbers or randomly deciding among equally performing numbers in your analysis, consider choosing higher numbers. A key concept lost on beginning players is that all numbers don't pay the same! At first glance, you're asking, "What?" But think about it. Prizes are split among all players who have the same winning numbers. Many players choose important dates in their lives like birthdays, anniversaries and other special occasions when choosing their numbers. This means they pick a lot of numbers in the 1-12 range, representing the months of the year. When you win, you want to win sharing the prize with fewer players.

6. Organize a group of players to pool resources so that you can cover many more combinations of numbers and tickets. Forming this syndicate, what I call the Big Wheel strategy, greatly increases everyone's chances of winning. You'll have to split the winnings, but is anyone going to complain if you hit the jackpot? Okay, there are complainers everywhere. Contemplate their moaning while you go mansion shopping.

7. Play more numbers and more tickets. For example, if you play seven numbers in a six-ball game, playing every one of the seven combinations reduces the odds from 1 in almost 14 million to 1 in 1,997,688. The more numbers you capture in your wheels, the more you reduce the odds of winning. This applies not just to the big monster prize, but to all the small prizes as well. By choosing every combination of eight numbers, which would be 28 tickets, your odds now drop to one in 499,422. Still real long, but you're getting closer.

17

10 MORE VALUABLE PLAYING TIPS

Here is a summary of 10 valuable playing tips, some of which I haven't discussed earlier, some that bear repeating, but all of them important considerations if you're serious about maximizing your profits in lottery and lotto games.

Without further ado:

1. Don't lose your tickets! That could prove disastrous if you get a big piece of a drawing or even hit the big one. Don't just chuck them on a counter filled with other papers and things. Put your tickets in a safe place where you always know to look. That way, when you want to find your tickets, you know *exactly* where they are.

2. Claim your winnings right away. You only have so long to collect your prize. There have been many occasions in the past where a winner waited so long to collect his winnings the prize was no longer valid. For example, if you are given one year to collect and show up one day late, you're out of luck. The rules are the rules. If you got it, go get it!

3. If you win big, stay away from the hucksters that will bombard you. And don't get overwhelmed by the sudden interest in you by distant family members and friends who come out of the woodwork like termites.

4. Consider the Big Wheel strategy, forming lottery syndicates with friends and colleagues to get a wider net of possible winnings. You'll have to split prizes but you're getting numbers and tickets you wouldn't have played otherwise. You can still play your own separate group of tickets outside the group if you want to.

5. When choosing between two games, go for the one that better suits your temperament or goals. Maybe it's the game with better odds of winning, maybe it's the game with more frequent payouts on the whole, maybe it's the game with the bigger jackpot, or maybe it's simply the game you like more for whatever reason, known or unknown. The most important concept here: Play the game that makes you the most comfortable or gives you the greatest enjoyment.

6. If your only goal is to win a monster jackpot, the ridiculously long odds really don't matter. You're already aware of the astronomical odds anyway, so astronomical odds in one game compared to more astronomical in another game may not make much difference when you're just shooting for life-changing money. That's why you're playing the game. You're dreaming big and it's hard to get swayed from the dream. If you were just thinking about the odds, you wouldn't play these games to begin with.

7. Play more tickets to increase your winning chances.

8. Play multiple games to get more action. But if you are risking too much weekly on games, do the opposite—play fewer games to restrict your action.

9. If you play a lot of lottery games, save all your ticket stubs. If you played $350 and won a $3,000 prize, that $3,000 will be taxable. However, you can write off the $350 expense on your taxes. Unfortunately, if you never win, the $350 in tickets is a loss that cannot be written off. Keep your tickets organized in a folder or a drawer specifically earmarked for this purpose.

10. Most important of all, have a plan, have a strategy.

18

PRACTICAL WISDOM & FURTHER THOUGHTS

Here are some questions and answers to help guide you in your quest to understand and beat the lottery:

1. WHAT IS THE BEST STRATEGY FOR WINNING MONEY?

Well, I've just devoted an entire book to this! But just the same, let me give you a simple answer.

While the question is straightforward, the answer is not necessarily quite that direct. Just as chess players choose from an array of hundreds of named opening moves to achieve their goals in the beginning of a match, so too do lottery players choose from a smorgasbord of strategies that offer their own advantages and disadvantage. Pugilists have different styles of outmaneuvering their opponents; baseball pitchers hurl a baseball in a variety of speeds, spins and locations to achieve their ends; comedians embrace different routines to make their audience laugh; and teachers use varying techniques to deliver their message. Professionals that specialize in their craft employ different strategies, methods and ways of going about it. These same concepts apply to lottery and lotto players.

So what is the best strategy for beating lottery or lotto games?

It is a matter of personal style. You have to choose a strategy or set of strategies that makes sense to you and that you can get behind. You've learned a multitude of core strategies, keys and exotic Level III strategies. All of them are powerful. You also have a choice of more advanced Level III strategies that are advertised in the back of this book and you can go online to www.lotterysupersystem.com for a further edge. All the options discussed in this book have their advantages and disadvantages. Ultimately, the best strategy for you is the one you feel most comfortable playing.

2. HOW DO I CHOOSE GAMES?

You can only directly buy lottery tickets in the state where the tickets are physically offered. You can always play lotteries in other states by having friends or family buy tickets but you'd better be able to trust them! If they physically have the ticket in their hands and claim the prize, you're going to have a difficult time getting your rightful jackpot if they don't want to give it to you. Money does strange things to people. It won't be the first time—or the hundredth time—this has happened.

There are lotteries on the Internet, but you would be a fool to play ones not run by a legitimate government. The game not only might be crooked, giving you absolutely zero chance of winning a jackpot—and you have no protections against that at all—but if you're lucky enough to win, it doesn't mean the operators will pay you the money. You have no legal recourse to collect your prize if it is not forthcoming. You also have the further issue of gambling across state lines, or even federal lines, which could be construed as an illegal activity. Playing the lottery or lotto might fit right into those murky waters.

You're pretty much limited to the games you can physically get to. If you're near a state border, you may have the choice of playing games in a nearby state.

But let's say you have the choice between a three-ball or four-ball daily game and a six-ball game. How do you decide?

First you need to establish your goals. If the only thing you care about is winning a huge jackpot, then you stick to the game that offers the monster prize for choosing the right numbers, typically a six-ball variation or dual-pool game. If you're looking for action and want to be in play while still chasing life-changing jackpots, then play all games available. The daily games will keep you in action while the bigger games will keep you in the dream.

You often don't have choices in the games offered by states around you unless, of course, you live near a border, but you'll often be offered multiple choices within your state. Just remember your goals. If your goal is to hit it rich in one mighty blow, make sure to play the game that affords you that opportunity. In other words, don't fool around with nickel-and-dime scratch-off games whose major prize won't change much in your life. Save your extra budget for games where a big win would change your world. Go for the gusto!

Whatever game or games you choose, go in there with a strategy. A real strategy. Go in with a plan. It makes the game much more enjoyable and separates you from the birthday, anniversary, shot-in-the-dark crowd.

3. HOW MUCH SHOULD I SPEND ON TICKETS EACH WEEK?

Your budget for lottery tickets is entirely up to you. You can spend as little as $10 per week to get the full power of the strategies in this book, though of course you increase your chances of hitting a jackpot by playing more tickets based on:

    a. Playing more aggressive strategies with more chosen numbers and keys.

    b. Getting more coverage of your chosen numbers, that is, buying more tickets.

    c. Playing aggressive Level II and Level III strategies

I have tried to drum this all-important concept into your head throughout the book and I won't miss this opportunity either— money management! Do not bet more than you can financially or emotionally afford.

Play the number of tickets you are comfortable playing and never, never count on potential winnings to pay your bills, nor should you take money away from necessities to play lottery games. That would be just plain foolish.

4. HOW QUICKLY CAN I EXPECT RESULTS FROM THESE STRATEGIES?

Hopefully you'll get winning results on the very first ticket— the power of *Lottery Super System* is always there—but you must understand that it is impossible to predict results on any particular drawing or group of drawings.

That is the nature of any game where chance is involved, from poker and blackjack to lottery and lotto, to really anything in life where elements of luck and the unknown are in play.

5. A FRIEND OF MINE TOLD ME ABOUT A RELATIVE WHO SAYS HE HAS A FOOLPROOF METHOD OF BEATING THE LOTTERY. HOW DOES HE DO IT?

He doesn't. He's just another blowhard in fantasyland. I've seen an endless parade of these fools through my life. They never lose at blackjack. They never lose at roulette. They always win at the horse track. They have a foolproof plan for beating the lottery. They win at least $1,000 every time they play craps. Excuse me while I throw up.

The ones who claim never to lose are the ones wearing pant legs that are either three inches too long or three inches too short.

6. IF I FOLLOW YOUR STRATEGIES, DO YOU GUARANTEE SUCCESS?

I wouldn't guarantee success for you no matter what you did in life, and certainly not when you're dealing with games containing large built-in negative expectations. It is difficult to win at anything that is speculative and where you're shooting for a longshot. It is difficult enough to win in casinos, and it is even more difficult to beat the lottery. But some people do. I'm hoping to make you one of that select group of winners.

7. TELL ME ABOUT LESSER-CHOSEN COMBINATIONS

When multiple players have the winning numbers, the jackpot will be split among all winning tickets. Thus, if you hit the big one and someone else has the identical number combination, that big prize gets split equally between you and the other fortunate winner.

What if you want to minimize the chances of that occurring?

Simple: If you are *not* working with a strategy and are just playing random numbers like everyone else, the safest way to protect your potential return is to avoid numbers that everyone else picks. Since many people play the dates of special days in their lives, you stay away from them, meaning that you avoid the numbers 1 through 12, the numerals of the months, unless your strategy dictates otherwise.

What happens if you win the lottery and, as an exaggeration, have to share the winning numbers with 99 other people? That would be a huge disappointment. Let's say the prize was $500,000. You jump up and down screaming with joy only to find out that you are sharing your birthday numbers with a ton of other people who liked those dates, 99 to be exact. You got a nice win, $5,000, but compared to half a million dollars that $5,000 is a pittance. Cancel the new car, cancel the down payment on a new house, and cancel the first-class hotel on your vacation. Stick with the three-star lodgings.

Splitting the jackpot too many times is bad news for you because you want to eat that whole stack of pancakes by yourself. With as much syrup as you want.

The other thing you can do is to pick combinations that superstitious players avoid. A perfect combination, if you don't mind it, is the so-called sign of the devil, 6-6-6. Okay, you don't like that number either. But find numbers that others avoid and you're less likely to share jackpots if you do hit.

8. WHERE ELSE CAN I LEARN ABOUT THE LEVEL II STRATEGIES, LEVEL III STRATEGIES, AND KEY NUMBERS?

Nowhere else. Key numbers, Level II strategies and Level III strategies are my exclusive work and there is no information anywhere else on them—at least not before I wrote this book and put it into the public spotlight. You have a few Level III strategies in this book, and can learn more about them by purchasing the advanced strategies in the back of this book.

9. WHAT IS THE BEST LOTTERY PREDICTION SOFTWARE ON THE MARKET?

Don't be silly! That's like throwing me a softball nice and easy and saying, "Swing, batter, swing!" Of course, I am partial to all the work I did on lotterysupersystem.com, but you'll see when you get to the site that there is nothing like it anywhere. You get the results of every major U.S. lottery and lotto game, including the big dual-pool games like Powerball and Mega Millions, plus you'll enjoy automated core strategy analysis for each of these games so that wherever you play, lottery-superstem.com has full coverage of your local game. There is a lot of great stuff on this site, perfect for casual and serious players alike, but I'll let the site do all the talking.

19

BEATING LOTTERY AND LOTTO WITH YOUR COMPUTER

If you're serious about beating the lottery, there really is only one way to crunch numbers so that you can get at the sweetmeat inside the nut, and that is to enlist the help of a computer program designed specifically for beating lottery and lotto games. There are so many variables to track and so many results to tally—especially if you are going to use Level I, Level II and Level III strategies—that it can be incredibly time consuming to work lottery and lotto strategies without the help of specialized software.

If you have been charting results by hand, I don't have to tell you about the amount of work involved in this painstaking process, even if you are using burst strategies and running it short. And if you are running it solid, running it long, or tracking multiple lottery games, that is one big job! This is the computer age and with the help of a good program, you can obtain results in a matter of clicks, as opposed to a matter of many hours or even many days, depending upon the task.

Why track a wall of data with a chisel when specialized software will do *all* of it for you with one giant jackhammer?

For example, if your strategy calls for a regression analysis of 100 or 250 games, discovering best numbers, cold numbers, clusters and all the various kinds of streaks and patterns would be an enormous task for just pen and paper, especially when you consider all the types of results you would like to obtain from the data.

Lotterysupersystem.com automates the key Level I strategies and keeps track of just about every winning lottery and lotto result in the United States and some other jurisdictions. You can click on any state, from California and Oregon to Texas and Florida, and all the states in between, and you'll get the winning results of every game played at whatever regression level you need. That's a tremendous amount of vital information available in a click. Imagine trying to find all those results and not knowing where to go, especially if it is a different game that you haven't been following?

That's why I created lotterysupersytem.com. I had been creating designer strategies for serious lottery and lotto players for a long time. I also had been working on systems for casual players. Most of all, I loved to analyze the numbers and patterns and think of ways to beat lottery and lotto games. But no work could be done on lottery games by mathematicians like myself, or casual and serious players, without easy access to the results of past drawings that we all rely on.

Besides the difficulty of charting by hand, which is certainly a valid way to analyze games, it's a matter of the best use of your time. You are better off *analyzing* data rather than compiling it. You are better served asking the computer to do certain things for you and then figuring out the best way to parse and use the results. If nothing else, rather than killing endless hours compiling data easily displayed (or crunched) by software programs, you could concentrate your time on fine-tuning your strategy approach, interpreting and using the data in a more advantageous manner, or just spending time with other activities you enjoy.

I've shown you how to do everything by hand in this book, both so that you understand the guts of the thinking and how the strategies work, and so that you also can put a serious hurt on the lottery and lotto games you like to play. But clearly, going the old-fashioned route is not the most optimal, desirable or profitable way to play lottery and lotto.

You will still do a certain amount of hand figuring because the programs aren't set up for everything you need, but you'll have a really good helper by your side.

You need serious tools nowadays to attack the lottery and lotto. Luckily for you, there is the computer.

LOTTERY SUPER SYSTEM.COM

I've been around the game a long time and have studied the intricacies of lottery and lotto systems from every direction. My approach starts with math and ends with math because that is my background. My library at home is filled with books on that discipline, enough books on probability and statistics to choke a beginning math student's curiosity, along with tomes on chaos theory, game theory and the like. Okay, I love math and have been studying numbers for a long time. I still do. I've brought my knowledge and experience in these fields into the creation of lotterysupersystem.com to address the particular needs of serious players.

I've designed LotterySuperSystem.com so that you can analyze hundreds of games back into lottery history within seconds. A set of powerful tools, it lets you customize your favorite lottery and lotto games and analyze numbers according to criteria you've established. The goal is to enhance your lottery experience, add hours of enjoyment, and give you all the information you need to craft the best winning tickets possible. And then let luck take its course.

It's pretty easy to see what my program is all about. There is a free membership level and it allows you to access a lot of free information on lottery and lotto games, plus use some core strategies. Well, without further ado, I'll just say check it out and let www.lotterysupersystem.com harness its strength to help you along the way to winning jackpots.

20

GO WIN A JACKPOT!

We've covered a lot of material and, hopefully, you are a more informed and prepared player than you were before turning the first page of *Lottery Super System*. You should be ready and confident in your approach to beating lottery and lotto games with the full fury of your new knowledge. The strategies in this book are designed to give you a powerful arsenal of weapons to be used against any three-ball or four-ball lottery game, five-ball or six-ball lotto game, or dual-pool multi-state game you will play

I want to remind you to stay aggressive, but not overly so. Money management is of utmost importance and, as you have read innumerable times in this book, I can't stress that enough. Do not fritter away money that has better uses—like for food, medical needs and rent. Lottery is a form of gambling that offers very poor odds of winning. Don't lose sight of that. And don't let all those numbers jumble your brain. Life needs come first.

But with that disclaimer out of the way, if you're going to play the lottery games, play to win. And play to win big!

I hope you have learned a lot from this book, not just about strategies for going after medium, large and super jackpots, but about being practical with your money as you chase the dream. We went over a tremendous amount of material in this book—chosen numbers, Level I core strategies, Level II keys, Level III exotics, and so much more—opening the window to new levels of strategies you may never have known existed. You've also received a lot of practical advice and valuable insider tips about the game, and learned how to use regression levels, wheels and all sorts of analysis methods.

I've given you a lot to work with here. Play tough and try to take down the big one. My final words before you bet your next ticket?

Go win a jackpot!

GLOSSARY
OF IMPORTANT
TERMS & CONCEPTS

2by2: A multi-state dual-pool hybrid lottery game.

6/25 Game: A six-ball lotto game with a pool of 25 total balls from which six winning balls will be drawn.

6/49 Game: A six-ball lotto game with a pool of 49 total balls from which six winning balls will be drawn.

6/51 Game: A six-ball lotto game with a pool of 51 total balls from which six winning balls will be drawn.

6/54 Game: A six-ball lotto game with a pool of 54 total balls from which six winning balls will be drawn.

Abbreviated Wheeling System: See **wheel.**

Anchor Ball: The lowest numbered ball in a cluster.

Balls: The physical balls used in lottery games, each one designated with a number that, if drawn, is one of the winning numbers.

Best Number Analysis: A chart that draws on the raw information from a Positional Analysis or Frequency Analysis to show the frequency of occurrence of drawn numbers from a specified number of lottery games so that users can easily see the number of times each ball was drawn starting with the top performing number on the first line and proceeding down to the number that was drawn the least number of times.

Best Number Frequency Analysis: A chart that sorts the data from a Raw Frequency Analysis Chart by order of frequency with the best performing number, that is, the hottest, listed first, the second hottest number listed second, and so on.

Best Number: A numbers that was drawn at a greater frequency than randomness would suggest.

Bias: A tendency of certain events to occur at a greater or lesser frequency than pure randomness would suggest.

Big Luck: The most important lucky number used as a chosen number or key in a wheel of tickets.

Big Wheel: A pool of multiple players acting together as a syndicate to buy a block of tickets and share winning prizes.

Box Bet: A lottery ticket which wins if the three or four numbers chosen appear in any order—as opposed to a *straight ticket*.

Burst: A regression analysis of ten games or less.

Chain Ball: The highest numbered ball in a cluster.

Chosen Numbers: Numbers a player has chosen, through any of the analysis methods or thorough sheer randomness, to play in a lotto or lottery game.

Cluster Analysis: The science of charting and statistically identifying and analyzing balls that have shown a tendency to be drawn together.

Clusters: Groups of numbers that have been drawn together in an individual drawing. Also called **paired numbers** or **paired groups**.

Cold Court Number: The third most overdue number in an overdue analysis.

Cold Number: A numbers that was drawn at a lesser frequency than randomness would suggest. Also **Overdue Number**.

Cold-Cold Number: A chosen number or key that hasn't been drawn in the longest span of games—as opposed to most recently drawn—compared to other overdue numbers.

Cold-Ten Number: A number that has been less frequently drawn—compared to other overdue numbers—over the most recent period of ten drawings.

Combination Bet: In three-ball lottery, a bet on all six combinations possible for one three-digit number, in essence a six-ticket bet.

Confidence Level: As it sounds, a player's confidence—which will be backed by his investment in tickets—in a number. The greater a player's *confidence* in a chosen number, the more tickets he will play that number on compared to other chosen numbers.

Core Strategies: The powerful everyday strategies players use to beat lottery and lotto games. Also called **Level I Strategies**.

Correct Clusters Method: The correct method of identifying clusters that looks for balls drawn together anywhere in the same drawing, as opposed to the *Incorrect Method*, which only identifies balls drawn sequentially.

Court Number: The third-best performer in a best number analysis.

Decade: A block of ten drawings.

Decades Analysis: An analysis of data by blocks of ten drawings.

Dual Master Key: In a dual-pool game, to have two master keys in play—one in the single-ball pool and one in the five-ball pool.

Dual-Pool Game: A game which features two pools of numbers, one set from which five balls are drawn, and a second set from which one ball is drawn. Multi-state games such as Powerball and Mega Millions are dual-pool games.

Duke: In an overdue analysis, the least frequently drawn number (coldest) in a specified number of games.

Earl: In an overdue analysis, the second-least frequently drawn number in a specified number of games

Early Trends: Trends that have occurred in the first half of an analysis, for example, the first five decades (50 games) in a decade analysis of 100 games.

Exotics: Advanced Level III strategies that are known and used by an elite group of experienced players.

Five Ball Lotto Games: A lotto game with a pool, typically, of from 25 to 54 balls, that draws five balls and awards the jackpot to the player or players who correctly choose all five numbers, and smaller prizes to players who correctly choose four, three and sometimes two of the drawn numbers.

Four Ball Game: See **Four-Ball Lottery.**

Four Ball Lottery: A lottery game that features four separate containers from which an individual ball will be drawn for a total of four balls. Players must pick the exact order of all balls drawn to win the jackpot. For example, if the draw is 0-3-7-5, the winning ticket must have those four numbers in exactly that order.

Fourth: The fourth-best performing number in a best-number analysis.

Frequency Analysis: The science of charting and statistically analyzing the winning balls in lotto games from a specified number of previous drawings.

Frequency of Position Chart: A chart that lists the number of times each chosen number is being played among a group of tickets. For example, in a group of nine tickets, the 13 might be played 8 times, the 7 six times, and 21 five times.

Full Wheel: A wheeling system that includes every possible combination of chosen numbers, as opposed to an **abbreviated wheel** or simply, **wheel**.

Grouping: A group of two balls drawn together in a lottery or lotto game.

High Wizard: A number that ranks among the top five hot numbers in a 100 game best number analysis and also among the top five overdue numbers in a 25 game overdue analysis.

Hot Lotto: A multi-state dual-pool hybrid lottery game.

Hot Number: A number that is drawn at a greater frequency than randomness would suggest.

Hot-Five Number—a number that has been hot compared to other hot numbers over the most recent five drawings.

Hot-Hot Number: A chosen number or a key that has been the most *recently* drawn (as opposed to the first drawn) when compared to other hot numbers.

Incorrect Clusters Method: An incorrect method of identifying clusters that looks for balls drawn together sequentially as opposed to being drawn together anywhere in the same drawing, which is the correct method.

Instant Game: A lottery game with the results predetermined on the ticket so that after purchase the player can immediately verify whether he has won or lost. Also called a **scratch-off game**.

Jackpot: The very biggest money prize, signifying a huge amount of money, in a lottery or lotto game.

Key Numbers: The most important number or numbers among tickets played in a lottery or lotto game, ones that have a player's highest confidence and will get played more frequently than other chosen numbers.

King Key Number: See **King**.

King: The most frequently drawn number in a best-number analysis.

Letter Conversion Chart: A chart that assigns one letter to each chosen number so that the chosen numbers can be correctly inserted into a wheel template.

Level I Strategies: Powerful everyday strategies such as best number, overdue, and cluster analyses, which are used to identify the top performing numbers in a series of past lottery and lotto drawings, and as a basis to make winning tickets. Also called **Core Analyses**.

Level II Strategies: Strategies that identify the most important chosen numbers—or bring in numbers from outside that group—and treat these numbers in a more aggressive or *more important* fashion when forming tickets.

Level III Strategies: Strategies that combine Level I core strategies and Level II key numbers—or combine other advanced methods—as centerpieces to form straightforward or intricate strategies designed to beat lottery and lotto games. One type of Level III Strategies is called the **Exotics**.

Little Lotto: Lotto games that draw from a smaller pools of balls, such as 36 or 39 (as opposed to a larger pool of balls such as 49), and pick five balls.

Little Luck: The second-most important number in a lucky analysis, behind the **Big Luck** (the most important).

Lottery Termite: The family members, friends, leaches and low-lifes who try to get a piece of a jackpot winner's prize by any persuasion method possible.

Lottery Wheel: A system of distributing chosen numbers that gives players partial or full coverage of all their possible combinations such that a group of tickets can be played at a reasonable cost, that is, much less than if every combination were played. Also called an **abbreviated wheeling system**.

Lottery: A game that features separate bins each containing ten balls from which an individual ball will be drawn. Players typically pay $1 per ticket to play and must choose the exact order of all balls drawn to win the jackpot.

LotterySuperSystem.com: A user-friendly online program specifically programmed to identify all winning lottery and lotto drawings over a long period of time and to use that information to create powerful and advanced winning strategies designed to beat future drawings.

Lotto: A game with a pool of balls that draws five or six balls and awards the big jackpot to the player or players who correctly choose all those numbers correctly, plus smaller prizes to players who correctly choose some of those winning numbers. Players typically pay $1 per ticket to play and may play as many tickets as they choose.

Lucky Analysis: An analysis that gives players the freedom of inputting their own lucky numbers into the tickets they'll play.

Lucky for Life: A multi-state dual-pool hybrid lottery game.

Lucky Number: Any number that a player feels is lucky for him or her and chooses to play as a chosen number or key.

Major Key: The most important key number in a multiple key ticket group, but not played on every ticket.

Master Key: A key number played on every ticket.

Mega Millions: A large dual-pool hybrid lottery game offered in more than forty states that features two pools, one with white balls and one with gold balls, with the grand prize growing at times to hundreds of millions of dollars.

MegaHits: A multi-state dual-pool hybrid lottery game.

MegaPlier: A multiplier option offered in Mega Millions that gives players, for $1 more, the chance to multiply their potential winning prizes by 2x, 3x, 4x and 5x. The Megaplier does not apply to the jackpot, only to the lesser prizes.

Minor Key: The second most important number in a multiple key ticket group.

Money Management: A strategy used by players to preserve their capital, manage their wins, and avoid unnecessary risks and big losses.

Multi-state Game: A hybrid lottery games offered in multiple states that pool all the bets together to form a massive jackpot of prize money. Also called a **Dual-Pool** game.

Multiplier: An option offered in some dual-pool multi-states games such as Mega Millions and Powerball that gives players, for $1 more, the chance to multiply their potential winnings on the smaller prizes by 2x, 3x, 4x, 5x and sometimes 10x. The multiplier does not apply to the jackpot.

Numbers: Any of the various balls, represented by numbers, in a pool of balls that have been drawn in lottery and lotto games, or that could be drawn.

Overdue Analysis: An analysis that refines data from Frequency Analysis or Positional Analysis charts that identifies numbers that have been the least frequently drawn over a specified number of games.

Overdue Frequency Analysis: A chart that sorts the data from a Raw Frequency Analysis Chart by order of frequency—the opposite of a Best Number Frequency Analysis—with the best performing number, that is, the most overdue (coldest) first, the second most overdue number second, and so on down to the hottest numbers.

Overdue Numbers: Numbers that have been the least frequently drawn over a specified number of games.

Overwheeling: Playing too many tickets or spending too much money on lottery and lotto games.

Paired Groups: See **Clusters.**

Paired Numbers: See **Clusters.**

Pari-Mutuel Game: A game where the total amount bet, less money taken by the government for its fees and costs, gets placed in the prize pool.

Pick 3: A three-ball lottery game with fixed prizes.

Pick 4: A four-ball lottery game with fixed prizes.

Plays: Tickets purchased in a lottery or lotto game.

Position: The bin in lottery—first, second, third or fourth (if a four-ball game)—from which a ball is drawn. For example, in a three ball game, first position indicates the bin from which the first ball is drawn, second position indicates the bin from which the second ball is drawn, and third position represents the bin from which the third ball is drawn.

Positional Analysis Raw Chart: A worksheet of raw data for lottery games that keeps track of the frequency of drawings for each ball by position.

Positional Analysis Refined Chart: A chart that translates the dots in a Positional Analysis Raw Chart into numbers such that the frequency of drawings for each digit in a lottery over a specified regression level can be determined at a glance.

Positional Analysis: The science of charting and statistically identifying and analyzing balls *by position* from a specified number of previous lottery games in which each ball gets drawn from a different bin.

Positional Drawing History: A chart that shows the date of drawing and the balls selected for each drawing, by position, over a specified number of lottery drawings.

Power Play: An extra bet in Powerball that can made for $1—it must be purchased at the time Powerball tickets are purchased—that allows players to increase their potential prize amounts (except for the jackpot) by a multiple of 2x, 3x, 4x, 5x or 10x.

Powerball: A large dual-pool hybrid lottery game offered in more than forty states that features two pools, one with white balls and one with red balls, with the grand prize growing at times to hundreds of millions of dollars. Also, the name of the ball drawn from the red pool.

Promotion: The elevation of a chosen number to a key, meaning it will be played on more tickets than the standard chosen numbers.

Quadrant Analysis: An analysis of data by blocks of twenty-five drawings.

Queen: The second-most frequently drawn number in a best-number analysis.

Raw Frequency Analysis Chart: A chart that displays the frequency of winning lotto balls from a specified number of previous drawings.

Recent Trends: Trends that have occurred in the last quarter or so of drawings—or quadrant, in a quadrant analysis.

Regression Analysis: An analysis over a specified number of prior lottery or lotto drawings.

Regression Level: A specified number of prior lottery or lotto drawings,

Repeating Clusters: Two numbers that get drawn together in two or more drawings over a specified number of games.

Rotating Master Key: Where a master key in one group of a dual-pool game, either the 1-ball group or the 5-ball group, is replaced by a different master key such that two identical groups of numbers—except for two different master keys—are played.

Run it Long: A regression level of 150 or more games.

Run it Short: A regression level of 11-50 games.

Run it Soft: A regression level of 51-99 games.

Run it Solid: A regression level of 100-149 games.

Scratch-off Tickets: A lottery game featuring instant results in which the user scratches off a covering on a paper ticket to determine if he has won a set prize amount.

Side Luck: The third-most important number in a lucky analysis.

Six-Ball Game: See **Six Ball Lotto**.

Six-Ball Lotto: A lotto game with a pool, typically, of from 25 to 54 balls, that draws five balls and awards the big jackpot to the player or players who correctly choose all five numbers, and smaller prizes to players who correctly choose five, four, three and sometimes two of the drawn numbers.

Straight Bet: In lottery games, a bet to pick the winning number in the *exact order* drawn.

Straight/Box Bet: In lottery games, a bet that the ticket played comes in exactly as picked or in any order (a straight bet plus a box bet) as long as it contains the correct numbers drawn. (This is actually a two-ticket play.)

Strategy Profile: A chart that displays the basic information you'll use to form a wheel including the game played, type or types of strategies being used, the pool of chosen numbers, the keys used, and the number of tickets being played.

Third Key: The third most important number in a multiple key ticket group.

Three Ball Lottery: A lottery game that features three separate containers from which an individual ball will be drawn for a total of three balls. Players must pick the exact order of all balls drawn to win the jackpot. For example, if the draw is 2-9-0, the winning ticket must have those three numbers in exactly that order.

Ticket: A slip of paper representing a bet on a lottery or lotto game.

Tri-State Megabucks Plus: A multi-state dual-pool lottery game.

Unbalanced Random Weighting: A group of tickets in which some numbers are played much more frequently than others without any strategic purpose.

Underwheeling: Playing fewer tickets than warranted based on a group of strong chosen numbers.

Weighting Numbers: To play some numbers more than other numbers in a group of tickets.

Wheel Template: A template that matches letters of a wheeling system with a player's chosen numbers so that wheels with good coverage of these numbers are created.

Wheel: A system of strategically distributing chosen numbers that gives a player partial coverage of all possible combinations such that a group of tickets can be played at a reasonable cost.

Wheeling System: See **Wheel.**

Wild Card 2: A multi-state dual-pool hybrid lottery game.

Wizard: A number that ranks among the top ten hot numbers in a 100 game best number analysis and also among the top ten overdue numbers in a 25 game overdue analysis.

Master Lotto and Lottery Strategies
-Prof. Jones' Winning Methods For Non-Computer Users-

Now, for the **first time** anywhere, learn Prof. Jones' **exclusive** Lotto and Lottery advanced **winning** systems. This package is chock-full of **powerful information** designed to give you an edge like never before!

It's time to play the Lotto and Lottery like a **pro** using Prof. Jones latest **scientific winning** systems.

Look at what you get -

50 WHEELING SYSTEMS

That's right, **50** advanced Dimitrov Wheeling Systems! You'll be playing with the most powerful lotto and lottery winning systems ever designed. These brilliant and revolutionary **winning systems** can be used successfully by anyone!

FREE AUTOMATIC WHEELING TEMPLATE AND INSTRUCTION GUIDE

Prof. Jones' **exclusive** automatic reusable plastic wheeling template is **included free** with your package and allows you to automatically record winning numbers. Also included is a specially written instruction guide that shows you how to use the wheeling systems and the templates provided.

Spend **only several minutes a day** inputting past winning numbers into the master templates and this **amazing system** quickly and **scientifically** generates the numbers that have the **best chances** of making you rich.

BONUS AND EXTRA BONUS!

Order now and receive 10 master Positional Analysis templates **and** 10 master Frequency Analysis templates, **absolutely free** with your order!

To order, send $24.95 by check or money order to:
Cardoza Publishing, P.O. Box 98115, Las Vegas, NV 89193

Pro-Master II Lotto and Lottery Strategies
- Prof. Jones' Ultimate Winning Strategy For <u>Non-Computer</u> Users -

Finally, after years of research into winning lotto tickets, Prof Jones has developed the ultimate in **winning jackpot strategies** for non-computer users! This **new power-house** gives you the **latest** in winning lotto strategies!

EASY TO USE - MINUTES A DAY TO WINNING JACKPOTS!

These **scientific winning systems** can be used successfully by anyone! Spend only **several minutes a day** inputting past winning numbers into the master templates and this **amazing system** quickly and **scientifically** generates the numbers that have the **best chances** of making you rich.

THE MASTER LOTTO/LOTTERY STRATEGIES AND MORE!

All the goodies of the <u>Master Lotto/Lottery</u> strategies - the winning systems, instruction guides, clear working template and bonus templates - are included in this **powerful winning strategy**, plus such **extra** features as the 3-Ball, 4-Ball and 6-Ball Sum Total charts. You also receive...

100 WHEELING SYSTEMS

That's right, **100** advanced Dimitrov Wheeling Systems - **double** the systems of the excellent <u>Master Lotto/Lottery</u> package! You'll be using the **most powerful** lotto and lottery winning systems ever designed.

BONUS

Included **free** with this **super strategy** are 15 Positional Analysis templates, 10 each 3-Ball, 4-Ball and 6-Ball Sum Total Templates and 15 Best Number templates!

EXTRA BONUS

Order now and you'll receive, **absolutely free** with your order, the extra bonus, <u>7 Insider Winning Tips</u> - a conside guide to **extra winning strategies**!

$50.00 Off! This $99.95 strategy is now <u>only $49.95 with this coupon</u>!

To order, send ~~$99.95~~ $49.95 plus postage and handling by check or money order to:
<u>Cardoza Publishing</u>, P.O. Box 98115, Las Vegas, NV 89193

FIVE BALL LOTTO WHEELS
Prof. Jones' Winning Strategy for Non-Computer Users

Five Ball Lotto Wheels

SPECIAL 5-BALL STRATEGY PACKAGE

For **5-ball lotto players**, this special package **gives you the master strategy** five ball wheels that allow you to play your **best numbers** and go for the big wins that other players dream about! **Popular and powerful**, these wheels get you ready for the action.

30 WHEELS INCLUDED

A **wide variety of wheels** covers bets for all situations, from **5 game plays** with a variety of best numbers, to wheels covering **24 game plays**, and others covering more than 20 of best number picks.

You'll find wheels such as 7 numbers-12 plays (7/12), 11/3, 19/18, 6/6 and 25 more great wheeling combinations to cover all your needs.

OTHER FEATURES

The 5-Ball Lotto Wheels Strategy Kit also contains **20** 5-Ball Lotto Sum Templates, a **clear Template** for ease-of-use in wheeling your best numbers, and a **5-Ball Lotto Sum chart** to provide a range of numbers and a guide in number-choosing strategies to help you win.

BONUS - Wheeling instructions included!
To order, send $25 by check or money order to: <u>Cardoza Publishing</u>

7 ADVANCED STRATEGY REPORTS TO WIN HUGE LOTTERY & LOTTO JACKPOTS

50% OFF — FIRST SERIES LOTTERY EXOTIC STRATEGIES

The First Series Lottery Exotic Strategies contains seven advanced booklets aimed at winning huge jackpots at lottery and lotto games—the Black Papers, Green Papers, Blue Papers, Red Papers, Orange Papers, Yellow Papers, and Purple Papers. Each strategy sells individually for $50, or $350 for the entire series of seven booklets.

From 20-30 pages each of **hard-hitting information**—no basic information here—you get access to the **most advanced** lotto and lottery strategies ever designed. These **exclusive strategies** are **not available anywhere else**! Imagine if you **win $10 million** or even **$100 million** and your investment was just $50! Start **winning now** by using the strongest strategies ever formulated. Good for all lottery and lotto games in the U.S., Canada, and the world, including multi-state games like Powerball & Mega Millions.

50% Off Bonus!!! Readers of *Lottery Super System* get 50% off with this coupon. You can order by mail (below), use the coupon online at our website or order by phone!

LEVEL III NORTH-SOUTH BI-POLAR STRATEGIES
The Purple Papers —$50 $25

These **powerful bi-polar plays** leave nothing to chance at both ends of the spectrum *You can have it both ways!* You learn how to **maximize opportunities** by playing hot and cold numbers simultaneously! Some players swear by hot numbers, others are aficionados of overdue plays. But there are astute players who don't quite like committing all their plays in one direction and are looking for a strong bi-polar blend. The Purple Papers have the answer! There are a **ton of strategies** here—pure hot-cold plays, weighted plays, bi-polar key strategies, unbalanced bipolar strategies, and reversed strategies.

Free Bonus: The Purple Papers include the following **FREE bonus strategy**: You also receive, **free**, the **very exclusive** Zone Strategies. These **powerful plays**—only available here—will give you a new set of plays to **attack jackpots!**

50% OFF SPECIAL!!!
Take 1/2 Off Any Strategy Package Combination!!!

Black Report: $25   Blue Report: $25   Red Report: $25
Green Report: $25   Purple Report: $25   Orange Report: $25
Yellow Report: $95   **Buy All Reports: Only $175! (50% OFF!)**

To order, send $350 $175 for all seven reports (or $25 per report)—plus P/H to:
Cardoza Publishing, P.O. Box 98115, Las Vegas, NV 89193

252